Challenges For Web Intelligence

Fabrice V. Riera

COPYRIGHT

First published in COUNTRY AND DATE

Copyright © Fabrice V. Riera

All rights reserved. No part of this publication may be reproduced, stored in a retrieval system or transmitted in any form or by any means without the prior permission in writing of the publisher, nor be circulated in writing of any publisher, nor be otherwise circulated in any form of binding or cover other than that in which it is published without a similar condition including this condition, being imposed on the subsequent purchaser.

To Benjamin and Nathan.

CONTENTS

Preface

    Foreword

    Why no Chapters

    Author Biography

    Bibliography/references

    Copyrights

    Why no chapters

    Trademarks

    Pre-requisite

    Limit of liability / Disclaimer of warranty

Challenges

    Challenge 1 Retrieving alphabetical values.

    Challenge 2 Retrieving columns.

    Challenge 3 Finish line.

    Challenge 4 Time difference in hours minutes and seconds

    Challenge 5 How to truncate time from a datetime

    Challenge 6 First day of last week

    Challenge 7 First day of current week

    Challenge 8 Last Working Day of Current Week

    Challenge 9 Last Day of Previous Week

    Challenge 10 First day of previous month

    Challenge 11 Last day of previous month

    Challenge 12 First day of current month

    Challenge 13 Last day of current month

Challenge 14 First day of current year

Challenge 15 Last day of current year

Challenge 16 First day of previous year

Challenge 17 Last day of previous year

Challenge 18 Calculating a linear regression

Challenge 19 Counting only valid records

Challenge 20 Adding continental locations to cities

Challenge 21 Highest quarterly sales for each year

Challenge 22 Highest monthly sales for each year

Challenge 23 Year with the highest sale

Challenge 24 Highest monthly sales over three years

Challenge 25 Highest quarterly sales over three years

PREFACE

Foreword

Since the author left SAP a few years ago, he found very difficult to keep his Business Objects skills as sharp as he would like.

Therefore the author started a training program to resurrect some old knowledge.

Nevertheless, practising on a daily basis without the perspective of sharing with the community, made the training days lacking some appeal.

Consequently, the author decided to keep track of his own practices by publishing them on his own web site.

Bibliography/references

The main concern when starting this book was to find resources. Resources were acquired from onsite experiences, internet and form other books.

Linear regression: http://www.gulland.com/wp/?p=534

Forums:
- www.forumtopics.com/busobj/index.php
- http://www.developpez.net/
- https://www.sdn.sap.com/irj/sdn/businessobjects-forums.

Books: SQL Puzzles & Answers (First edition) / Joe Celko

Why no chapters and no page numbers?

The book will be organized in "Challenges" instead of being organised in chapters, The reason is that "Challenges" gives much more flexibility and avoid the trap of unbalanced chapters.

Because of technical issue at the time of the publication, the book will be presented without page numbers. However the challenge numbers should be sufficient to guide the reader through the reading.

Copyrights

All rights reserved. No part of this publication may be reproduced, distributed, or transmitted in any form or by any means, including photocopying, recording, or other electronic or mechanical methods, without the prior written permission of the author Fabrice V. Riera, except in the case of brief quotations embodied in critical reviews and certain other non-commercial uses permitted by copyright law. For permission requests, write to the author at the email address below: mail@apachegeek.com. In the subject enter: "Requesting Permissions".

Trademarks

Business Objects and the Business Objects logo, Business Objects, Crystal Reports, Crystal Decisions, Web Intelligence, XCelsius, and other Business objects products and services mentioned herein as well as their respective logos are trademarks or registered trademarks of SAP AG, Dietmar-Hopp-Allee 16, 69190 Walldorf, Germany. Business Objects is a SAP Company.

SAP Business Objects Screen shot, graphics and data used in this book are subject to copyright of SAP AG, Dietmar-Hopp-Allee 16. 69190 Walldorf, Germany.

Microsoft Windows, Microsoft Access, Microsoft SQL Server, Microsoft Excel, Microsoft Word, Microsoft PowerPoint, Microsoft Office and Microsoft Notepad are trademarks of Microsoft Corporation.

Adobe, the Adobe logo, Acrobat, Postscript, and the reader are either trademarks or registered trademarks of Adobe Systems Incorporated in the United States and /or other countries.

All other products mentioned are registered or unregistered trademarks of their respective companies.

Pre-requisite

This book is not a training guide explaining in a detailed way the web intelligence functionalities, but rather a web intelligence mind teaser. This book presumes that the reader has already assimilated the web intelligence functionalities, or is at least aware of them.

All the challenges listed in this book have been tested with SQL server and as well with web intelligence XI R3.

The data samples used in this book can be easily recreated or found in the "efashion" universe.

Each tab is divided in three parts as shown below:

- **Challenge:** Contains the description of the challenge.
- **Expected Result:** Provide the expected result.
- **Solution:** Display the steps toward a resolution.

Limit of liability and Disclaimer of Warranty

The Author and Publishers of this information have made their best effort to provide a high quality and informative book. No representations or warranties of any kind are made with regard to the accuracy, applicability, fitness or completeness of the contents of this book.

The Author and Publishers accept no liability of any kind for any losses or damages caused, or alleged to be caused, directly or indirectly from using any of the information contained in this book.

The Author and Publishers disclaim any warranties (expressed or implied), merchantability, or fitness for any particular purpose.

Author's web site

Other products can be found at the author's web site .www.apachegeek.com

Email address : mail@apachegeek.com

Retrieving alphabetical value

 ## Challenge

Business requirement: You have been provided with a database sample containing "dirty data" and have been requested to build a first report based on the table below.

This report will demonstrate how to eliminate the presence of nulls and numbers.

The business has required the issued to be dealt with at query panel level.

First Name	Last Name
Jim	Kirk
Paul	Anderson
Null	Morrison
111	Goodyear

Business justification: Aggregated data can be significantly affected by relatively small amounts of dirty data, all the more if the expected output is a ratio or a percentage.

Business clue: The where clause of your query must be able to select only characters.

Reference: Joe Celko / SQL Puzzle and Answers (First edition).

 ## Expected Result

First_Name	Last_Name
Paul	Anderson
Jim	Kirk

 ## Solution

1. Let's presume that you have already created a universe with two dimensions "First_Name" and "Last_Name".

2. Start the creation of a new report and target your universe.

3. Select the dimensions "First_name" and "Last_Name".

4. In the Query Filter panel set your condition as shown below.

   The filter put in place will affect only the characters located between the first letters and the last letter of the alphabet.

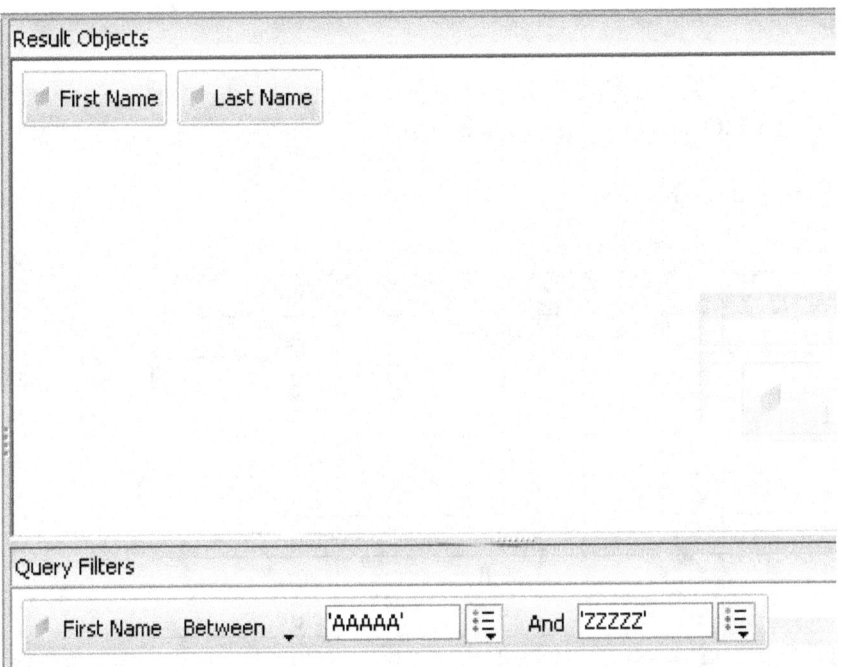

5. Run the query. As you can see, only the characters are selected.

First Name	Last Name
Jim	Kirk
Paul	Anderson

Pivoting columns

Challenge | 2

Challenge

Business requirement: You have been assigned the responsibility to group the same family of values belonging to "Q_OptionID" and "Q_ans_text" into a unique row.

You will use the table below as a reference.

ID	Clientid	Surveyid	Question ID	Q_OptionID	Q_ans_text
1	1	1	1	Null	Yes
2	1	1	2	18	Null
3	1	1	3	19	Null
4	2	1	1	Null	No
5	2	1	2	18	Null
6	2	1	3	19	Null
7	3	2	1	Null	Yes
8	3	2	2	15	Null
9	3	2	3	13	Null

Business justification: The readability of a table is affected if it does not let you narrow down a data set or analyze relationships between data points.

Business Clue: The suggested solution is to create a reversed pivot table to summarize, analyze, explore and present your data under a new angle.

Expected Result

Clientid	Surveyid	Q1	Q2	Q3
1	1	Yes	18	19
2	1	No	18	19
3	2	Yes	15	13

Expected Solution

The best thing to do is to compartmentalize the difficulties and progress step by step toward a resolution.

1. First of all, create a derived table in the semantic layer based on the table above.

   In this derived table, you will use a UNION ALL to put into the same column the values that you want to gather inside the same row.

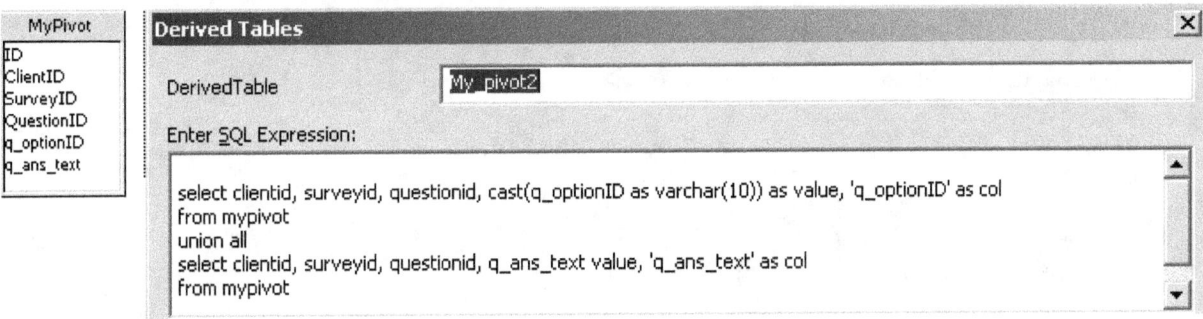

2. Create a class folder "My_pivot2".

3. Add the corresponding dimensions belonging to your newly derived table in your universe.

4. Export your universe.

5. From Info view, start a new report based on "My_pivot2".

6. Drag and drop the appropriate dimensions in the result panel.

7. Create three variables

- Q1

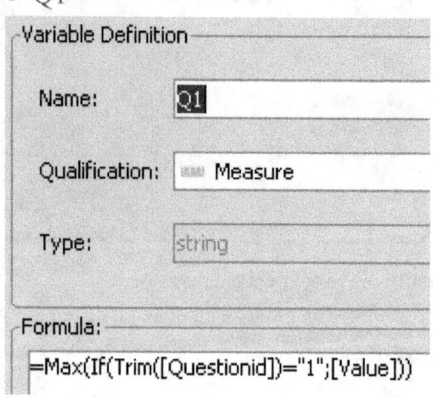

Sample code:

```
=Max(If(Trim([Questionid])="1";[Value]))
```

- Q2

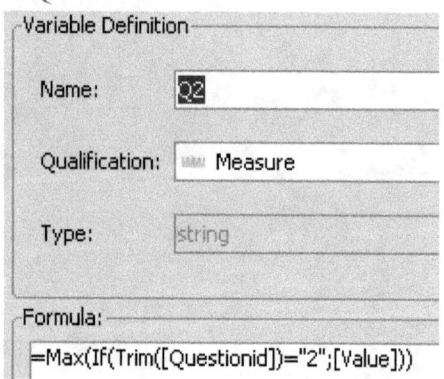

Sample code:

```
=Max(If(Trim([Questionid])="2";[Value]))
```

- Q3

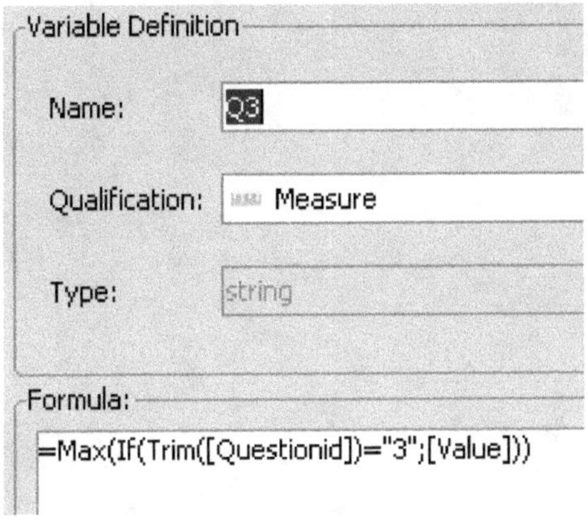

Variable Definition

Name: Q3

Qualification: Measure

Type: string

Formula:
=Max(If(Trim([Questionid])="3";[Value]))

Sample code:

```
=Max(If(Trim([Questionid])="3";[Value]))
```

8. Remove the columns "QuestionID", "Value", Col.

9. Create three columns next to "SurveyID".

10. Drag and drop into the three newly added columns, the three following objects in a sequential order: "Q1","Q2", "Q3".

   Your table should appear as shown below:

Clientid	Surveyid	Q1	Q2	Q3
1	1			
1	1		18	
1	1			19
1	1	Yes		
1	1			
1	1			
2	1			
2	1		18	
2	1			19
2	1	No		
2	1			

11. Select your table format and go to the properties.

12. If the box "Avoid Duplicate Row Aggregation" is checked, then uncheck it.

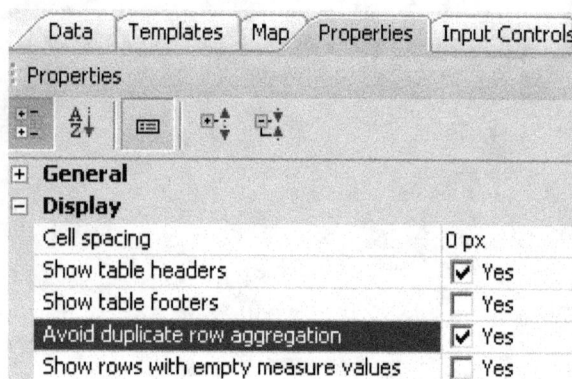

13. The result should be displayed as shown below without any duplicated row.

Clientid	Surveyid	Q1	Q2	Q3
1	1	Yes	18	19
2	1	No	18	19
3	2	Yes	15	13

Finish Line

Challenge 3

Challenge

Business requirement: The business provides you with a sample of data in the table below. This sample of data contains records which can be grouped by "Sport Event".

First Name	Last Name	Sport Event	Finish Line
Joe	Stone	Roller	NULL
Joao	Andrew	Karate	1
Victor	Lapierre	Footbal	3
Charlene	Denis	Boat	NULL
Paul	Kirk	Karate	NULL
James	Chy	Football	NULL

You are requested to produce a report retrieving the participants having passed the finish line but you are requested to ignore those who did not pass the finish line.

However in some cases the "Sport Event" column does not contain anybody having passed the "Finish Line", therefore regarding these specific "Sport Event" you are allowed to select a participant with a NULL value.

If you have got any doubt regarding the requirement, refer to the **Expected Result** and just try to reproduce the table displayed

Business justification: Proof of Concept

Business Clue: You will need to compartmentalize your solutions by creating different queries and then by cross checking these queries.

Reference: Joe Celko / SQL Puzzle and answers

Expected result

First Name	Last Name	Sport Event	Finish Line
Joe	Stone	Roller	NULL
Joao	Andrew	Karate	1
Victor	Lapierre	Footbal	3
Charlene	Denis	Boat	NULL

Solution 1

1. First of all, create in your universe the dimensions
   "First_Name", "Last_Name", "Sport_Event", "Finish_Line".

2. Export your universe.

3. Start the creation of a report based on the dimensions "First_Name", "Last_Name", "Sport_Event", "Finish_Line".

You should get the same result as shown below.

First Name	Last Name	Sport Event	Finish Line
Charlene	Denis	Boat	
James	Chy	Football	
Joao	Andrew	Karate	1
Joe	Stone	Roller	
Paul	Kirk	Karate	
Victor	Lapierre	Football	3

4. Put a section on "Sporting Event".

Boat			
First Name	Last Name	Sport Event	Finish Line
Charlene	Denis	Boat	
		Boat	
Football			
First Name	Last Name	Sport Event	Finish Line
James	Chy	Football	

First Name	Last Name	Sport Event	Finish Line
Victor	Lapierre	Football	3
		Football	

Karate

First Name	Last Name	Sport Event	Finish Line
Joao	Andrew	Karate	1
Paul	Kirk		
		Karate	

Roller

First Name	Last Name	Sport Event	Finish Line
Joe	Stone	roller	

5. Create a variable "Count" as shown below.

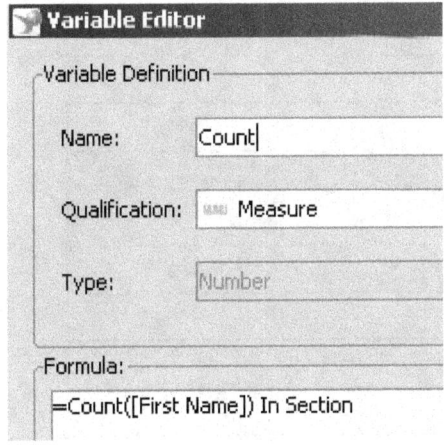

6. Create the variable "Hide/Show" as shown below.

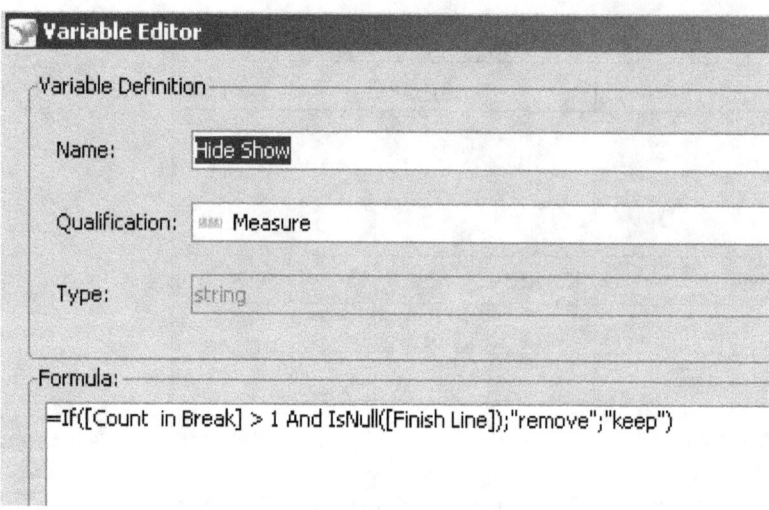

7. On the right side of your table, add a new column.

8. In this new column, drag and drop "Hide/Show".

You should get the following table.

Boat				
First Name	Last Name	Sport Event	Finish Line	Hide / Show
Charlene	Denis	Boat		Keep
		Boat		
Football				
First Name	Last Name	Sport Event	Finish Line	
James	Chy	Football		Remove
Victor	Lapierre	Football	3	Keep
		Football		
Karate				
First Name	Last Name	Sport Event	Finish Line	
Joao	Andrew	Karate	1	Keep
Paul	Kirk			Remove
		Karate		
Roller				
First Name	Last Name	Sport Event	Finish Line	
Joe	Stone	roller		Keep

10. Select the "Show/Hide" filter panel.

11. Drop into the filter editor the "Hide/Show" measure.

12. In the filter editor, type the value ''Keep'' as requested and then select it as shown in the screen shot below.

11. Your report should display the table below.

Boat				
First Name	Last Name	Sport Event	Finish Line	Hide / Show
Charlene	Denis	Boat		Keep
		Boat		
Football				
First Name	Last Name	Sport Event	Finish Line	
Victor	Lapierre	Football	3	Keep
		Football		
Karate				
First Name	Last Name	Sport Event	Finish Line	
Joao	Andrew	Karate	1	Keep
		Karate		
Roller				
First Name	Last Name	Sport Event	Finish Line	
Joe	Stone	roller		Keep

Solution 2

Another solution can be provided at query panel level.

However, the web intelligence query panel does not provide enough flexibility to write in one block a SQL statement resolving this challenge.

The solution would be to compartmentalize the problem and to build a set of queries:

- The first query would gather all the records having a NULL in "Finish Line".

- The second query would focus on selecting only the records having a not null value in the column "Finish Line".

- The third query would collect all the records having a NULL in "Finish Line" but would be filtered with the second query.

1. Create the first query and in the where clause set "Finish Line" is null.

    You are going to retrieve all the participant who did not cross the finish line.

2. Create the second query and in the where clause set "Finish Line" is not null.

With this query you are going to retrieve all the participants who passed the finish line

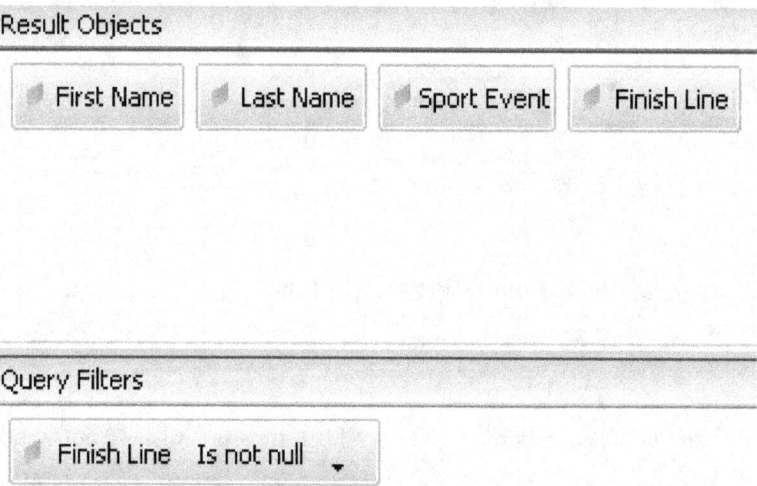

3. Create the third query but in the where clause, make sure that "Sporting Event" is filtered with the result of the second query.

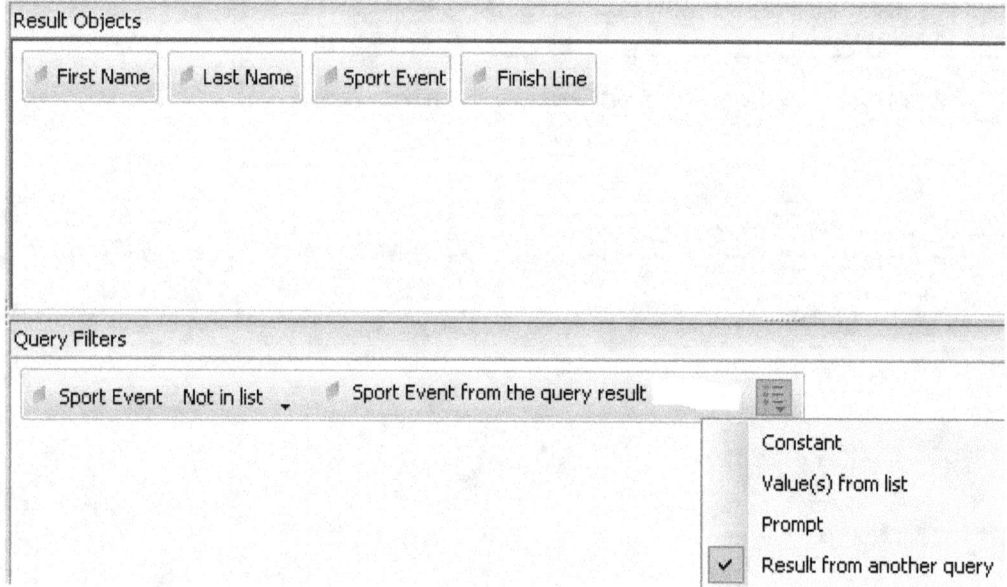

The query will provide you with the people by name who did not pass the finish line and whose sport event is not associated with anybody that might have passed the finish line.

Run the third query and see the result below

First Name	Last Name	Sport Event	Finish Line
Charlene	Denis	Boat	
Joe	Stone	Roller	

4. Now what we want to do is a union between the third query and the second query.

Combine the queries as shown in the screen shots below.

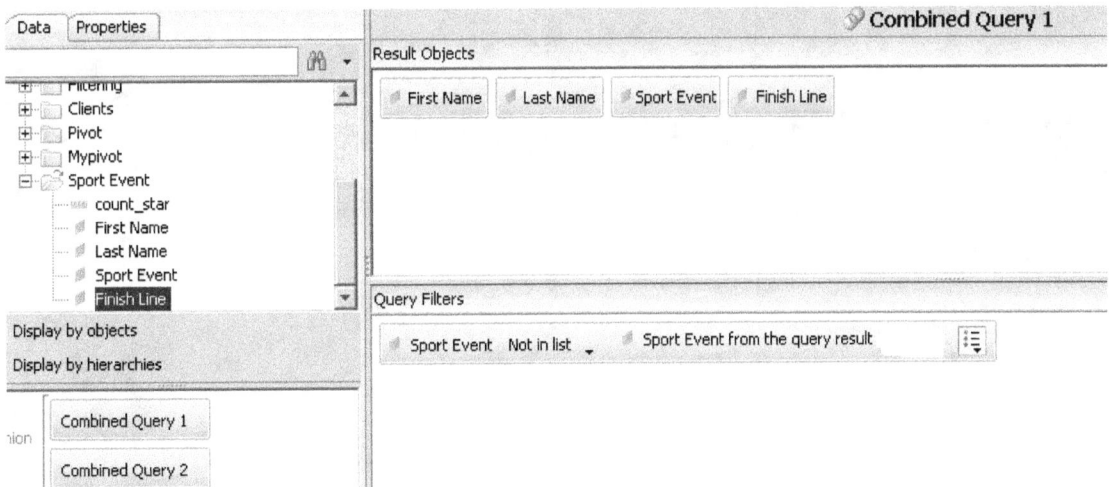

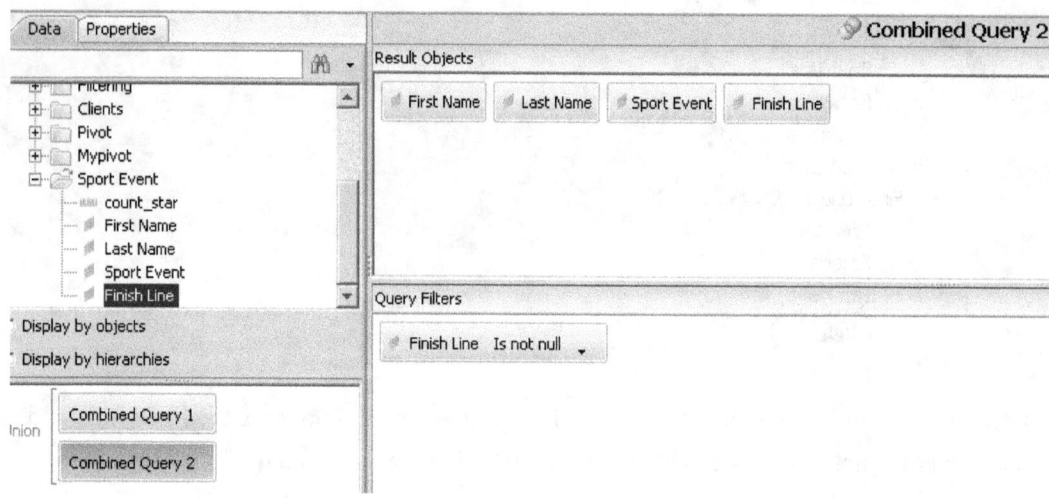

5. Run the query. You should get the result below:

First Name	Last Name	Sport Event	Finish Line
Charlene	Denis	Boat	
Joao	Andrew	Karate	1
Joe	Stone	Roller	
Victor	Lapierre	Football	3

Time difference in Hours Minutes and Seconds

Challenge | 4

Challenge

Business requirement: You are requested to create a report based on the table below showing the time spent by workers in a secured area.

Your report will involve calculation regarding the difference between a start time and end time in hours, minutes and seconds.

First Name	Last Name	Start Datetime	End Datetime
Annie	Fittipaldi	01/02/2012 01:02:25 AM	01/02/2012 01:10:57 AM
Fred	Lajoie	01/01/2012 01:02:25 AM	01/01/2012 01:06:25 AM
Maurice	Denis	01/01/2012 01:02:25 AM	01/01/2012 02:06:45 AM
Paul	John	01/01/2012 01:02:25 AM	01/01/2012 01:02:25 AM

Business justification: Scoring system down.

Business clue: You have been assigned the responsibility of recreating in web intelligence the table below, as displayed in "Expected result".

Reference: On site experience.

Expected Result

First Name	Last Name	Start Datetime	End Datetime	Time In Seconds	Time Conversion
Annie	Fittipaldi	01/02/2012 01:02:25 AM	01/02/2012 01:10:57 AM	512	00:08:32
Fred	Lajoie	01/01/2012 01:02:25 AM	01/01/2012 01:06:25 AM	240	00:04:00
Maurice	Denis	01/01/2012 01:02:25 AM	01/01/2012 02:06:45 AM	3860	01:04:20
Paul	John	01/01/2012 01:02:25 AM	01/01/2012 01:02:25 AM	0	00:00:00

Solution

This challenge can be resolved using the following steps:

- Calculating the difference between days in seconds.
- Calculating the difference between the hours, minutes and seconds, in seconds.
- Cumulating the two steps above
- Converting the whole output into hours, minutes and seconds.

2. Let's presume that you already have a universe with the dimension "First name", "Last Name", "Start datetime", "End datetime"

3. Create a report based on the objects above.

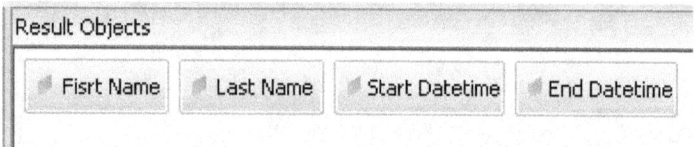

4. Create a measure that does the following:

   o Get the difference between days in seconds.

   o Get the difference between hours, minutes and seconds, in seconds.

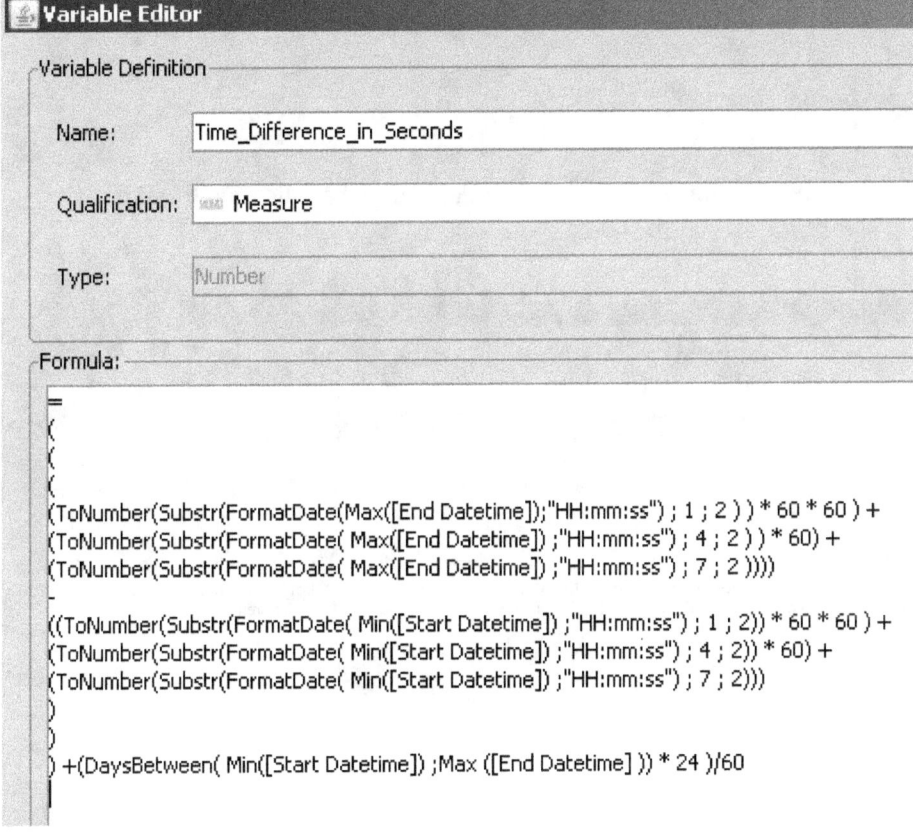

Code sample 1:

```
=

(
(
(
(ToNumber(Substr(FormatDate(Max([End Datetime]);"HH:mm:ss") ; 1 ; 2 ) ) * 60 * 60 ) +
(ToNumber(Substr(FormatDate( Max([End Datetime]) ;"HH:mm:ss") ; 4 ; 2 ) ) * 60) +
(ToNumber(Substr(FormatDate( Max([End Datetime]) ;"HH:mm:ss") ; 7 ; 2 ))))
-
((ToNumber(Substr(FormatDate( Min([Start Datetime]) ;"HH:mm:ss") ; 1 ; 2)) * 60 * 60 ) +
(ToNumber(Substr(FormatDate( Min([Start Datetime]) ;"HH:mm:ss") ; 4 ; 2)) * 60) +
(ToNumber(Substr(FormatDate( Min([Start Datetime]) ;"HH:mm:ss") ; 7 ; 2)))
)
)
) +(DaysBetween( Min([Start Datetime]) ;Max ([End Datetime] )) * 24 )/60
```

5. Create the "Time_Conversion" measure.

This measure will be used to turn the timeframe previously calculated into the following format: HH:MM: SS.

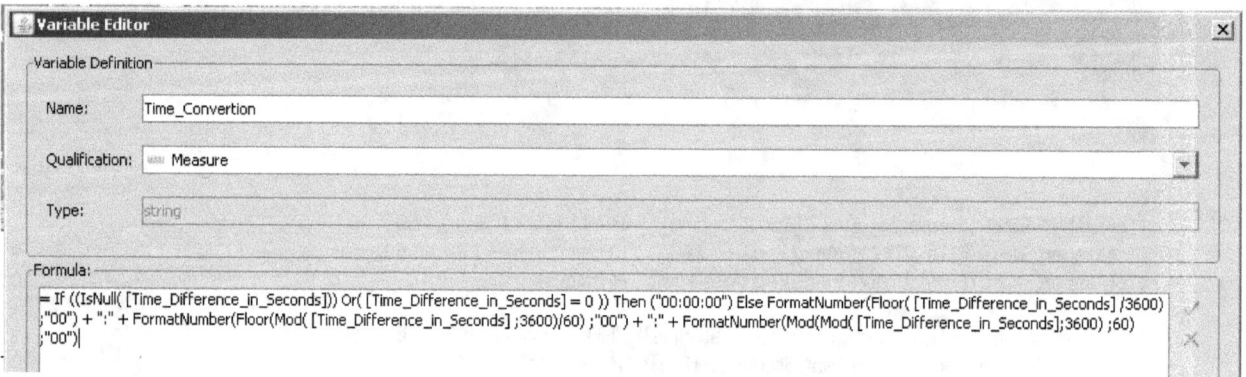

Code sample 2:

```
= If ((IsNull( [Time_Difference_in_Seconds])) Or( [Time_Difference_in_Seconds] = 0 )) Then
("00:00:00") Else FormatNumber(Floor( [Time_Difference_in_Seconds] /3600) ;"00") + ":" +
FormatNumber(Floor(Mod( [Time_Difference_in_Seconds] ;3600)/60) ;"00") + ":" +
FormatNumber(Mod(Mod([Time_Difference_in_Seconds];3600);60);"00")
```

6. Add two columns next to "End Datetime".

7. Drag and drop sequentially into these columns the two previously created objects: "Time difference in seconds" followed by "Time Conversion".

8. The result should be displayed as shown below:

First Name	Last Name	Start Datetime	End Datetime	Time Difference In Seconds	Time Conversion
Annie	Fittipaldi	01/12/2012 01:02:25 AM	01/01/2012 01:10:57 AM	512	00:08:32
Fred	Lajoie	01/01/2012 01:02:25 AM	01/01/2012 01:06:25 AM	240	00:04:00
Maurice	Denis	01/01/2012 01:02:25 AM	01/01/2012 02:06:45 AM	3860	01:04:20
Paul	John	01/01/2012 01:02:25 AM	01/01/2012 01:02:25 AM	0	00:00:00

How to truncate time from a Date time field

Challenge 5

🔍 Challenge

Business requirement: You have been requested to improve the readability of the "Start Date" column below by turning a datetime value into a date.

First Name	Last Name	Start Date	End Date
Paul	John	2012-01-01 01:02:25.0000000	2012-01-01 01:02:25.000
Fred	Lajoie	2012-01-01 01:02:25.0000000	2012-01-01 01:06:25.000
Maurice	Denis	2012-01-01 01:02:25.0000000	2012-01-01 02:06:45.000
Annie	Fittipaldi	2012-01-02 01:02:25.0000000	2012-01-02 01:10:57.000

Business justification: Improving readability.

Business clue: Formatting the date.

🔍 Expected Result

First Name	Last Name	Start Datetime	Date
Paul	John	2012-01-01 01.02:25.0	01/01/2012
Fred	Lajoie	2012-01-01 01.02:25.0	01/01/2012
Maurice	Denis	2012-01-01 01.02:25.0	01/01/2012
Annie	Fittipaldi	2012-01-01 01.02:25.0	01/01/2012

 Solution 1

1. Let's presume that a universe has already been created based on the sample table displayed above.

    This universe contains the following dimensions: "First Name", "Last Name", "Start Datetime".

2. Start a new report based on the dimensions above "First Name", "Last Name" and "Start Datetime".

3. Create a variable called "OnlyDate".

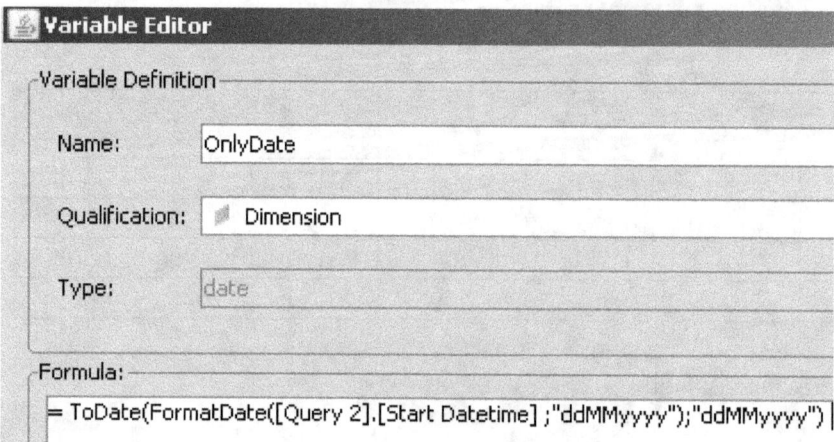

Code sample:

```
=ToDate(FormatDate([Query 2].[Start Datetime];"ddMMyyyy");"ddMMyyyy")
```

4. Create a new column next to "Start Datetime".

5. Drag and drop the variable "OnlyDate" in the new column. Only the date should appear in this new table.

Start Datetime	Only Date
01/02/2012 1:02:25 AM	01/02/2012
01/01/2012 1:02:25 AM	01/01/2012
01/01/2012 1:02:25 AM	01/01/2012
01/01/2012 1:02:25 AM	01/01/2012

Solution 2

1. Right click the column "Start Datetime".

Start Datetime
01/02/2012 1:02:25 AM
01/01/2012 1:02:25 AM
01/01/2012 1:02:25 AM
01/01/2012 1:02:25 AM

2. Select "FormatNumber".

3. As a "FormatType" select "Date/Time", then select "9/21/2004".

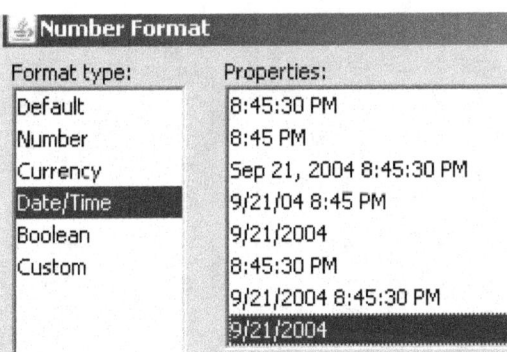

4. Click ok.

5. The result should be displayed as shown below.

Start Datetime
01/02/2012
01/01/2012
01/01/2012
01/01/2012

First day of last week

 Challenge

Business requirement: Creating reports based on days are quite common, all the more that such records can be exploited in many ways. In this challenge we will be **chasing** the first day of last week based on the table below.

Date
02/05/2013

Business justification: N/A.

Business clue: You have been assigned the responsibility of creating in web intelligence a report obtaining the same output as in the "Expected result".

In the "Expected result" if the day number is 2 (Tuesday), then we need to subtract from this day number the right amount of days to get the previous first day of last week which should be 8.

Reference: Forums.

Expected Result

Date	First day of the week before
02/05/2013	2/25/2013

Solution

We need first to find out the day number for the date "3/5/2013".

1. Start a new report based on the dimension Date.

2. Create another variable "First day of previous week".

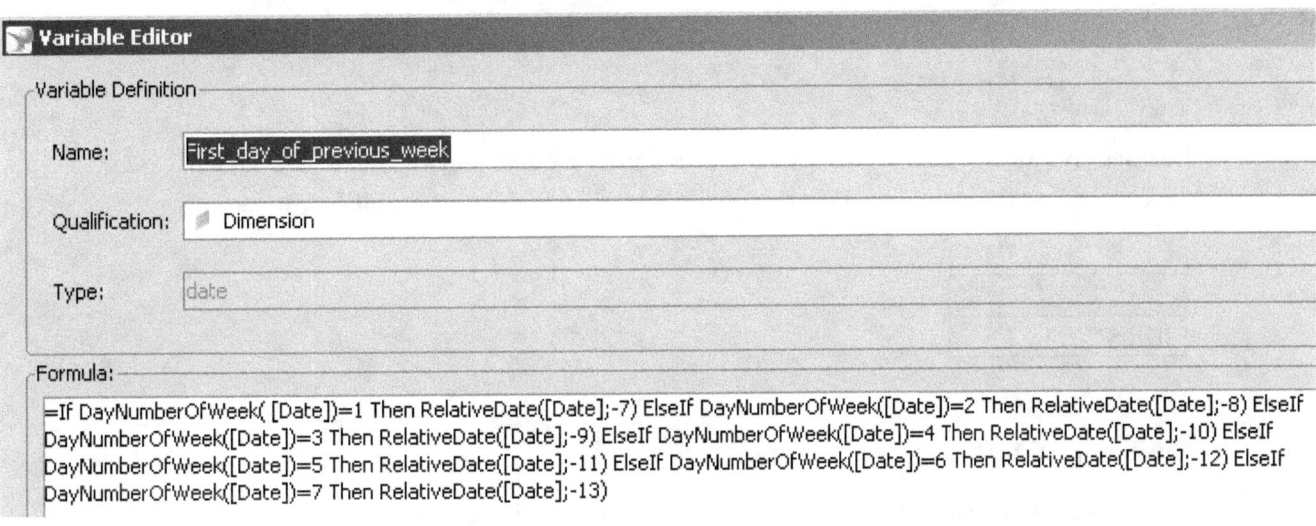

Code sample:

=IfDayNumberOfWeek([Date])=1 Then RelativeDate([Date];-7) ElseIf DayNumberOfWeek([Date])=2 Then RelativeDate([Date];-8) ElseIfDayNumberOfWeek([Date])=3 Then RelativeDate([Date];-9) ElseIfDayNumberOfWeek([Date])=4 Then RelativeDate([Date];-10) ElseIfDayNumberOfWeek([Date])=5 Then RelativeDate([Date];-11) ElseIf DayNumberOfWeek([Date])=6 Then RelativeDate([Date];-12) ElseIfDayNumberOfWeek([Date])=7 Then RelativeDate([Date];-13)

3. Add a new column next to "Date".

4. Drag and Drop "First day of previous week" into the new column and you should get the result as shown below.

Date	First day of previous week
03/05/2013	02/25/2013

First day of current week

Challenge | 7

 ## Challenge

Business requirement: This challenge is a continuation of the previous challenge but will explore the concept of "Extracting the First day of current week" based on the table below.

Date
02/05/2013

Business justification: N/A.

Business clue: You have been assigned the responsibility of creating in web intelligence a report obtaining the same output as in the "Expected result".

Reference: Forums.

 ## Expected Result

Date	First day of current before
2/5/2013	3/4/2013

 ## Solution

Similar to the previous example, we need first to find out the day number of the date "2/5/2013". In the example above the day number is 2 (Tuesday).

Then we need to subtract from this day number, the right amount of days to get the first day of the current week.

1. Start a new report based on the dimension Date.

2. Create a variable "First day of current week".

Variable Editor

Variable Definition

Name: First_day_of_current_week

Qualification: Dimension

Type: date

Formula:
=If DayNumberOfWeek(CurrentDate())=1 Then RelativeDate(CurrentDate();-0) ElseIf DayNumberOfWeek(CurrentDate())=2 Then RelativeDate(CurrentDate();-1) ElseIf DayNumberOfWeek(CurrentDate())=3 Then RelativeDate(CurrentDate();-2) ElseIf DayNumberOfWeek(CurrentDate())=4 Then RelativeDate(CurrentDate();-3) ElseIf DayNumberOfWeek(CurrentDate())=5 Then RelativeDate(CurrentDate();-4) ElseIf DayNumberOfWeek(CurrentDate())=6 Then RelativeDate(CurrentDate();-15) ElseIf DayNumberOfWeek(CurrentDate())=7 Then RelativeDate(CurrentDate();-6)

Code sample:

```
=If DayNumberOfWeek(CurrentDate())=1 Then RelativeDate(CurrentDate();-0) ElseIf
DayNumberOfWeek(CurrentDate())=2 Then RelativeDate(CurrentDate();-1) ElseIf
DayNumberOfWeek(CurrentDate())=3 Then RelativeDate(CurrentDate();-2) ElseIf
DayNumberOfWeek(CurrentDate())=4 Then RelativeDate(CurrentDate();-3) ElseIf
DayNumberOfWeek(CurrentDate())=5 Then RelativeDate(CurrentDate();-4) ElseIf
DayNumberOfWeek(CurrentDate())=6 Then RelativeDate(CurrentDate();-15) ElseIf
DayNumberOfWeek(CurrentDate())=7 Then RelativeDate(CurrentDate();-6)
```

3. Add a new column next to Date.

4. Drag and Drop "First day of current week" next to the Date column.

5. Your report should display the following result

Date	First day of current week
03/05/2013	03/04/2013

Last Working Day of Current Week

🔍 Challenge

Business requirement: This challenge is a continuation of the previous challenge but will explore the concept of "Last Working day of Current Week" based on the table below.

Date
02/05/2013

Business justification: N/A

Business clue: You have been assigned the responsibility of creating in web intelligence a report obtaining the same output as in "Expected result".

Reference: Forums.

🔍 Expected Result

If the current week is "2/5/2013" then the last working day of the current week will be "3/8/2013".

🎯 Solution

You need to use the function DayNumberOfWeek () and the function RelativeDate ().

The function DayNumberOfWeek () will give you the number of the day in the week and the function RelativeDate () will retrieve the last working day based on DayNumberOfWeek ().

1. Start a new report based on the dimension Date

2. Create a variable called "Last working day of current week".

Variable Editor

Variable Definition

Name: Last_working_day_of_current_week

Qualification: Dimension

Type: date

Formula:
=If DayNumberOfWeek(CurrentDate())=1 Then RelativeDate(CurrentDate();+4) ElseIf DayNumberOfWeek(CurrentDate())=2 Then RelativeDate(CurrentDate();+3) ElseIf DayNumberOfWeek(CurrentDate())=3 Then RelativeDate(CurrentDate();+2) ElseIf DayNumberOfWeek(CurrentDate())=4 Then RelativeDate(CurrentDate();+1) ElseIf DayNumberOfWeek(CurrentDate())=5 Then RelativeDate(CurrentDate();+0) ElseIf DayNumberOfWeek(CurrentDate())=6 Then RelativeDate(CurrentDate();-1) ElseIf DayNumberOfWeek(CurrentDate())=7 Then RelativeDate(CurrentDate();-2)

Code sample:

```
=IfDayNumberOfWeek(CurrentDate())=1 Then RelativeDate(CurrentDate();+4)
ElseIf DayNumberOfWeek(CurrentDate())=2  Then
RelativeDate(CurrentDate();+3)  ElseIf DayNumberOfWeek(CurrentDate())=3
Then  RelativeDate(CurrentDate();+2)  ElseIf
DayNumberOfWeek(CurrentDate())=4  Then  RelativeDate(CurrentDate();+1)
ElseIf DayNumberOfWeek(CurrentDate())=5  Then
RelativeDate(CurrentDate();+0)  ElseIf DayNumberOfWeek(CurrentDate())=6
Then  RelativeDate(CurrentDate();-1)  ElseIf DayNumberOfWeek(CurrentDate())=7
Then  RelativeDate(CurrentDate();-2)
```

3. Add a new column next to "Date".

4. Drag and drop "Last working day of current week" into the new column.

5. Your report should display an output as shown below:

Date	Last working day of current week
03/05/2013	03/08/2013

Last Day of Previous Week

Challenge

Business requirement: This challenge is a continuation of the previous challenge, but will explore the concept of "Last Day of previous Week" based on the table below.

Date
2/5/2013

Business justification: N/A

Business clue: You have been assigned the responsibility of creating in web intelligence a report obtaining the same output as in "Expected result".

Reference: Forums.

Expected Result

Date	Last day of previous week
03/05/2013	03/03/2013

Solution

1. Start a new report based on the dimension "Date".

2. Create a variable called "Last day of previous week".

3. Add a new column next to "Date".

4. Drag and drop this variable in the new column.

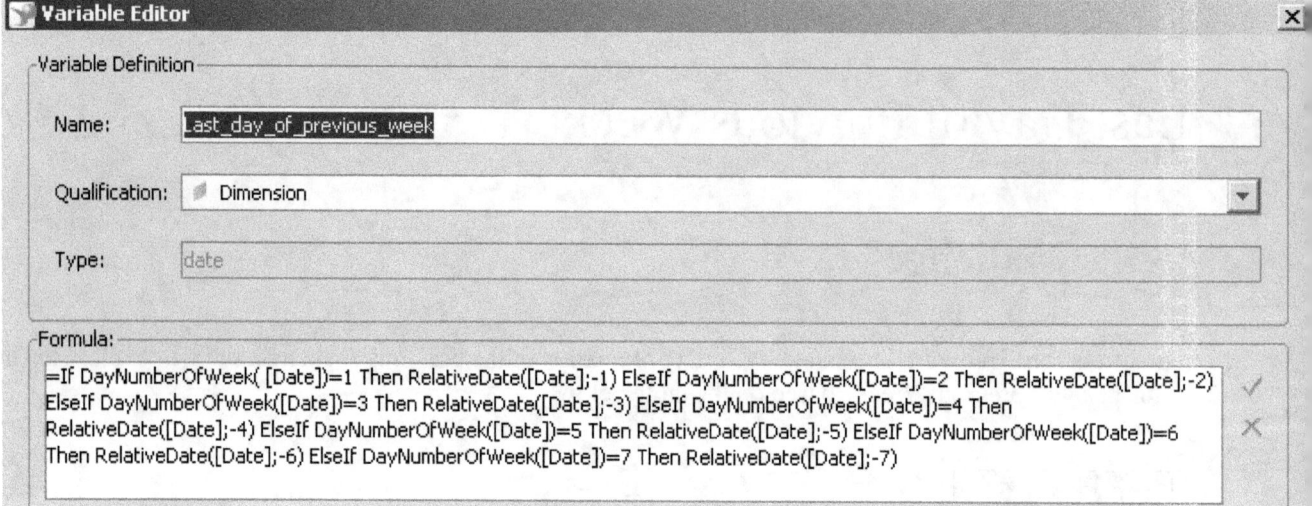

Code sample:

```
=If DayNumberOfWeek( [Date])=1 Then RelativeDate([Date];-1) ElseIf DayNumberOfWeek([Date])=2 Then RelativeDate([Date];-2) ElseIf DayNumberOfWeek([Date])=3 Then RelativeDate([Date];-3) ElseIf DayNumberOfWeek([Date])=4 Then RelativeDate([Date];-4) ElseIf DayNumberOfWeek([Date])=5 Then RelativeDate([Date];-5) ElseIf DayNumberOfWeek([Date])=6 Then RelativeDate([Date];-6) ElseIf DayNumberOfWeek([Date])=7 Then RelativeDate([Date];-7)
```

5. The report should display a result similar to the one below:

Date	First day of previous week
03/05/2013	03/03/2013

First day of previous month   Challenge | 10

🔍 Challenge

Business requirement: This challenge is a continuation of the previous challenge, but will explore the concept of "First day of previous month" based on the table below.

Date
02/05/2013

Business justification: N/A.

Business clue: You have been assigned the responsibility of creating in web intelligence a report obtaining the same output as in "Expected result".

Reference: Forums.

🔍 Expected Result

Date	First day of previous month
02/05/2013	02/01/2013

🏃 Solution

1. Start a new report based on the dimension Date

2. Create a variable called "First day of previous month".

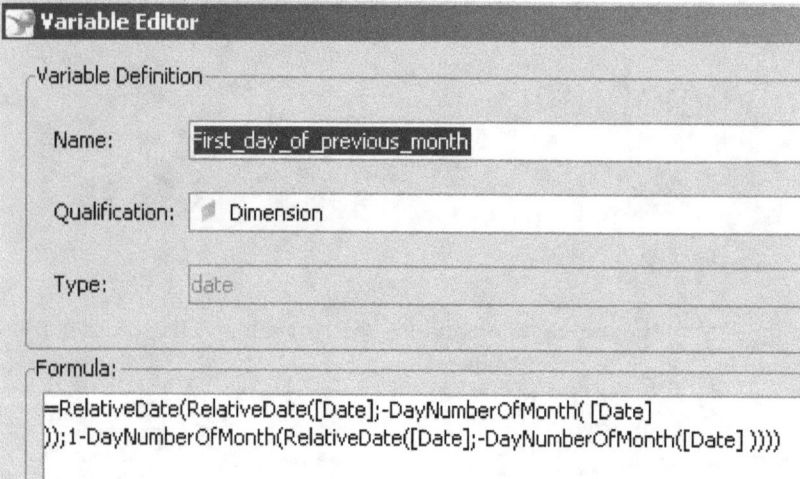

Code sample:

```
=RelativeDate(RelativeDate([Date];-DayNumberOfMonth( [Date] ));1-
DayNumberOfMonth(RelativeDate([Date];-DayNumberOfMonth([Date]  ))))
```

3. Drag and drop this variable next to Date.

4. The result below should be displayed:

Date	First day of previous month
03/05/2013	02/01/2013

Last day of previous month

Challenge | 11

🔍 Challenge

Business requirement: This challenge is a continuation of the previous challenge, but will explore the concept of "Last day of previous month" based on the table below.

Date
02/05/2013

Business justification: N/A.

Business clue: You have been assigned the responsibility of creating in web intelligence a report obtaining the same output as in "Expected result".

Reference: Forums.

🔍 Expected Result

If the current date given is 2/5/2013 then the output should be 2/28/2013.

Date	Last day of previous month
02/05/2013	2/28/2013

Solution

1. Start a new report based on the dimension Date.

2. Create a variable called "Last day of previous month".

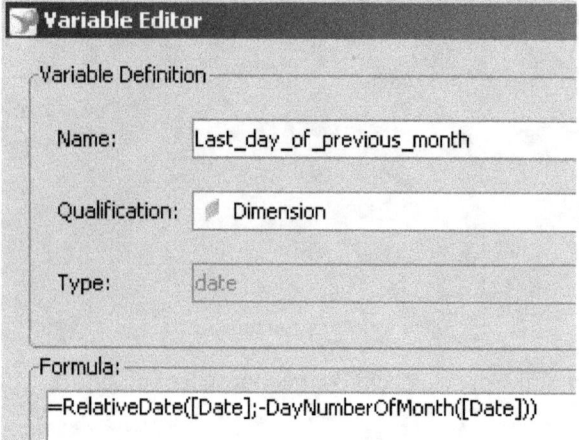

Code sample:

=RelativeDate(CurrentDate();-DayNumberOfMonth(CurrentDate()))

3. Add a new column, drag and drop this variable into the new column.

4. The result below should be displayed:

Date	Last day of previous month
03/05/2013	2/28/2013

N.B : The initial result was in fact 2/27/2013. The system was not able to display 28. The root cause was not identified but it is possible it could be a bug. Therefore I created a variable containing "2/28/2013" to replace the wrong result with the right one.

First day of current month

Challenge | 12

 Challenge

Business requirement: This challenge is a continuation of the previous challenge, but will explore the concept of "Last day of previous month" based on the table below.

Business justification: N/A

Business clue: You have been assigned the responsibility of creating in web intelligence a report obtaining the same output as in "Expected result".

Reference: Forums.

Expected Result

If the current date is "3/5/2013" then the output should be "3/1/2013".

Solution

1. Start a new report based on the dimension Date

2. Create a variable called "1st day of current month".

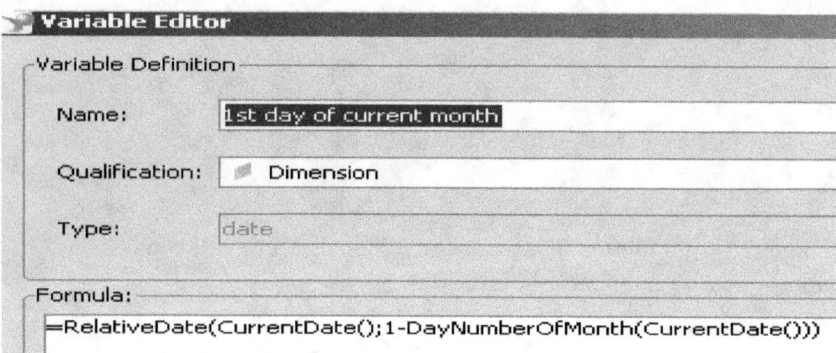

Code sample:

=RelativeDate(CurrentDate();1-DayNumberOfMonth(CurrentDate()))

3. Add a new column, drag and drop this variable into the new column.

4. The result below should be displayed as show below:

Date	1st day of current month
03/05/2013	03/01/2013

Last day of current month

Challenge | 13

 Challenge

Business requirement: This challenge is a continuation of the previous challenge, but will explore the concept of "Last day of current month" based on the table below.

Date
02/05/2013

Business justification: N/A

Business clue: You have been assigned the responsibility of creating in web intelligence a report obtaining the same output as in "Expected result".

Reference: Forums.

 Expected Result

If the current date given is "3/5/2013" then the output should be "3/31/2013".

Solution

1. Start a new report based on the dimension Date

2. Create a variable called "1st day of current month".

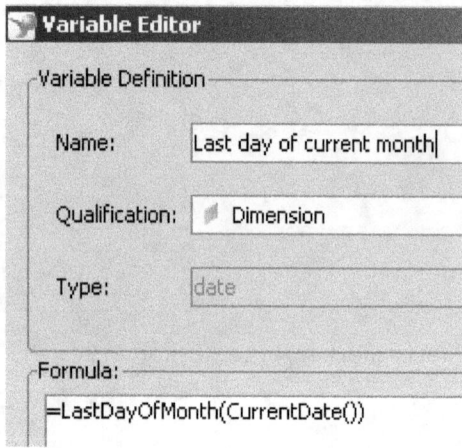

Code sample:

```
=LastDayOfMonth(CurrentDate())
```

3. Drag and drop this variable next to "Date".

4. The result below should be displayed:

Date	Last day of Current Month
03/05/2013	3/31/2013

First day of current year   *Challenge* | 14

Challenge

Business requirement: This challenge is a continuation of the previous challenge, but will explore the concept of "First day of current week".

Business justification: N/A

Business clue: You have been assigned the responsibility of creating in web intelligence a report obtaining the same output as in "Expected result".

Reference: Forums.

Expected Result

If the current date given is "3/5/2013" then the output should be "1/1/2013".

Solution

1. Start a new report based on the dimension Date

2. Create a new variable First day of current year.

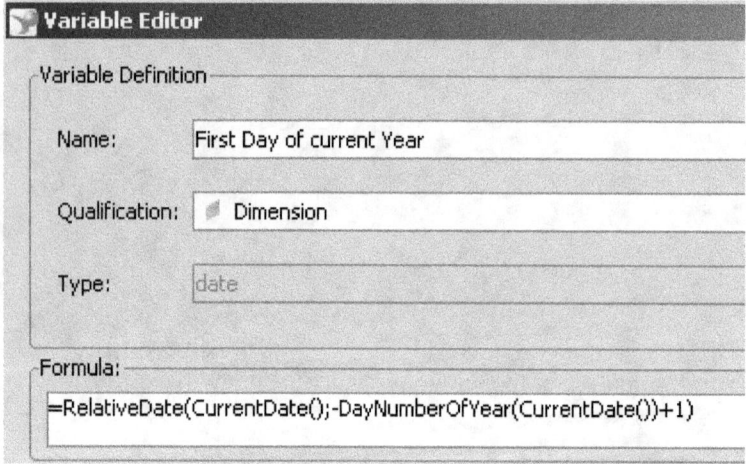

Code sample:

```
=RelativeDate(CurrentDate();-DayNumberOfYear(CurrentDate())+1)
```

3. Add a new column, drag and drop this variable into the new column.

4. The result below should be displayed:

Date	First Day of current year
03/05/2013	01/01/2013

Last day of current year

Challenge

Business requirement: This challenge is a continuation of the previous challenge, but will explore the concept of "Last day of current year".

Business justification: N/A

Business clue: You have been assigned the responsibility of creating in web intelligence a report obtaining the same output as in "Expected result

Reference: Forums.

Expected Result

If the current date given is "3/5/2013" then the output should be "12/31/2013".

Solution

The solution provided in this challenge will not be using the current date. I was unable to find a solution using the current date function, and will instead suggest a more practical answer.

1. Start a new report based on the dimension Date.

2. Create the variable below.

We are not going to get current year from the current date but instead we are going to concatenate this year with the last well known day and month of the current year.

The sign # will be used to turn 2,013 into 2013.

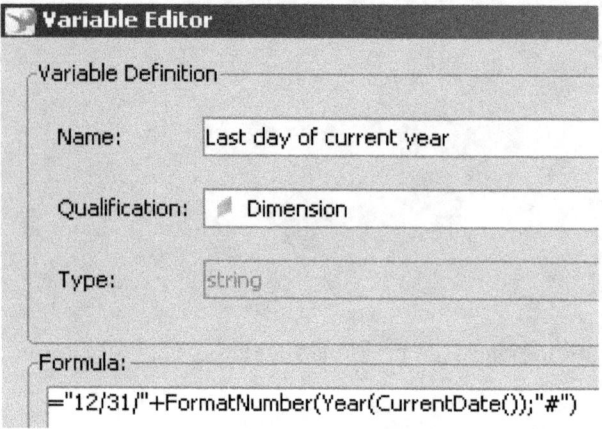

Code sample:

```
="12/31/"+FormatNumber(Year(CurrentDate());"#")
```

3. Create a second variable.

Remark 1: ToDate() function is needed to turn the concatenated date into a real date.

Remark 2: ToDate() function uses "MM" and not "mm" as may have been expected.

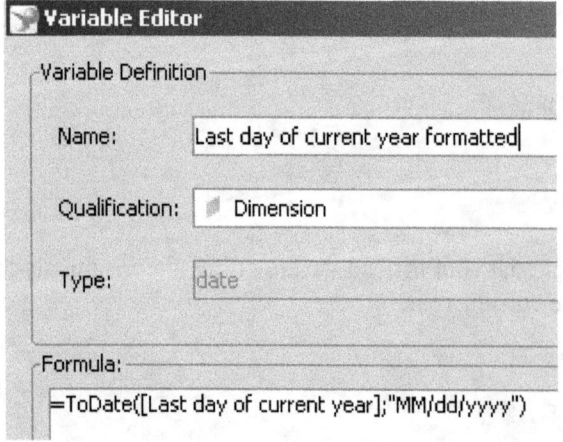

Code sample:

```
=ToDate([Last day of current year];"MM/dd/yyyy")
```

3. Drag and drop the dimension "Last date of current year formatted" next to the dimension Date.

5. You should get the result displayed below:

Date	Last day of current year
03/05/2013	12/31/2012

First day of previous year

Challenge | 16

 ## Challenge

Business requirement: This challenge is a continuation of the previous challenge, but will explore the concept of "First day of previous year".

Business justification: N/A

Business clue: You have been assigned the responsibility of creating in web intelligence a report obtaining the same output as in "Expected result.

Reference: Forums.

 ## Expected Result

If the date is "3/5/2013" then the first day of the previous year will be "1/1/2013".

 ## Solution

1. Create a report based on the dimension Date.

2. Create a variable "First day of previous year".

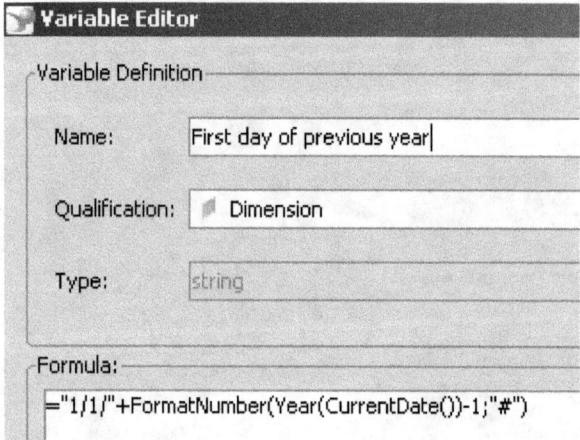

Code sample:

```
="1/1/"+FormatNumber(Year(CurrentDate())-1;"#")
```

3. Create another variable ''First day of previous year formatted''

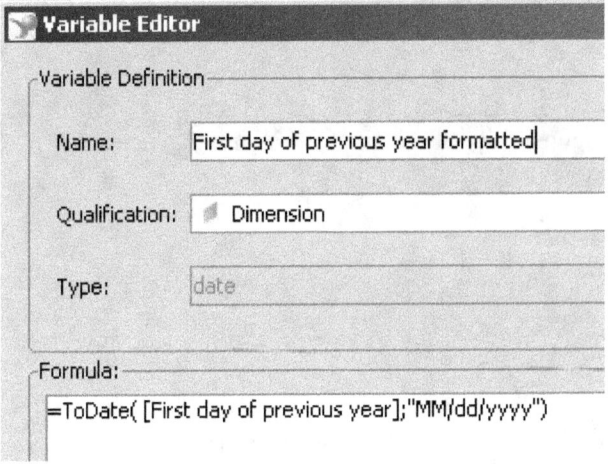

Code sample:

```
=ToDate( [Last day of previous year ] ;"MM/dd/yyyy")
```

4- Drag and drop this variable next to the dimension Date. You should get the result below:

Date	First day of previous year formatted
03/05/2013	01/01/2012

Last day of previous year   *Challenge* | 17

 ## Challenge

Business requirement: This challenge is a continuation of the previous challenge, but will explore the concept of "Last day of previous year".

Business justification: N/A

Business clue: You have been assigned the responsibility of creating in web intelligence a report obtaining the same output as in "Expected result.

Reference: Forums.

 ## Expected Result

If the date is "3/5/2013" then the first day of the previous year will be "1/31/2012".

 ## Solution

1. Create a new report based on the dimension Date.

2. Create the variable "Last day of previous year".

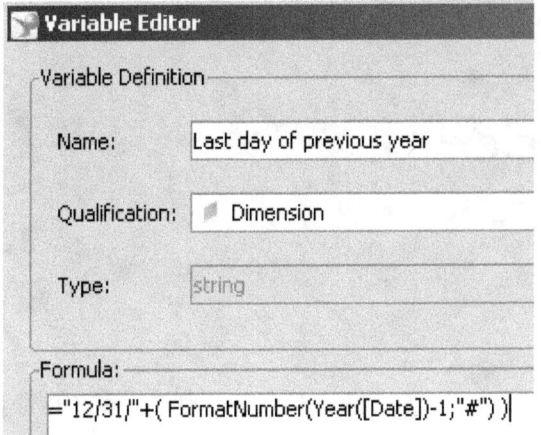

Code sample:

```
="12/31/"+( FormatNumber(Year(CurrentDate())-1;"#")   )
```

3. Create the variable "Last day of previous year formatted".

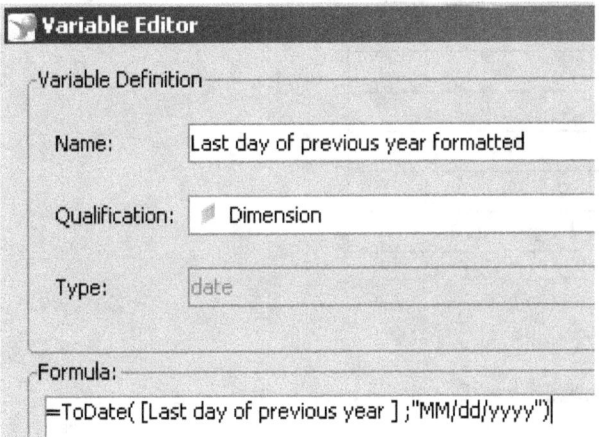

Code sample:

```
=ToDate( [Last day of previous year ] ;"MM/dd/yyyy")
```

4. Add a new column, drag and drop the variable "Last day of previous year formatted" next to the dimension Date.

Date	Last day of previous year
03/05/2013	12/31/2012

Calculating a linear regression   *Challenge* | 18

🔍 Challenge

Business requirement: The marketing department is requesting you to build a report showing the level of correlation between sunny days and the sale of sun glasses.

In order to answer such questions you need to establish the level of correlation between the sunny days and the sale of sun glasses based on the table below.

Sun Glasses Sold	Sunny days	Months
10	10	January
11	11	February
14	12	March
16	14	April
17	15	May
25	20	June
30	30	July
30	31	August
20	29	September
15	20	October
11	12	November
9	10	December

Business justification: N/A

Business clue: You have been assigned the responsibility of creating in web intelligence a report obtaining the same output as in "Expected result.

You will need to refer to the following web site: "http://www.gulland.com" in order to get the appropriate statistic tools.

Reference: Forums.

 **Expected Result**

N/A

 **Solution**

The best way to understand the dependency between values and to make some forecast would be to generate some linear analysis using a linear regression equation.

The linear regression formulas used in this demonstration has been found and developed by the following website: http://www.gulland.com/wp/?p=534

A first approach in term of linear analysis would involve the design of a chart using for the X axis: the number of sunny days and, for the Y axis: the number of sun glasses sales.

A more elaborate and formal way would be to create a linear regression equation involving the calculation of a covariance, a variance, a gradient and a correlation coefficient.

1. Create a report based on the dimension "Sun Glasses Sold", "Sunny days" and "Months".

2. Create the variable "x-avg(x)".

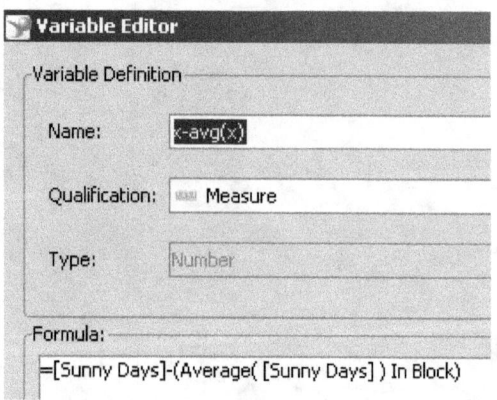

Code sample:

=[Sunny Days]-(Average([Sunny Days]) In Block

3. Create a variable "y–avg(y)"

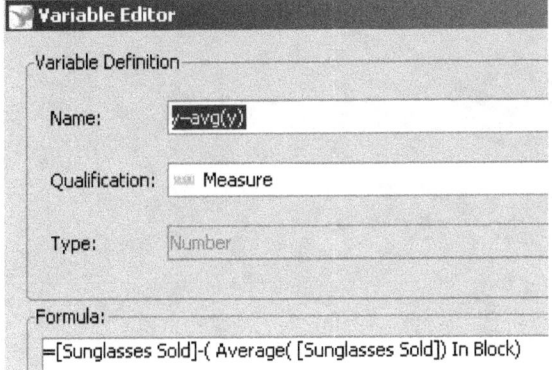

Code sample:

=[Sunglasses Sold]-(Average([Sunglasses Sold]) In Block)

4. Create a variable called "Covariance" as shown below:

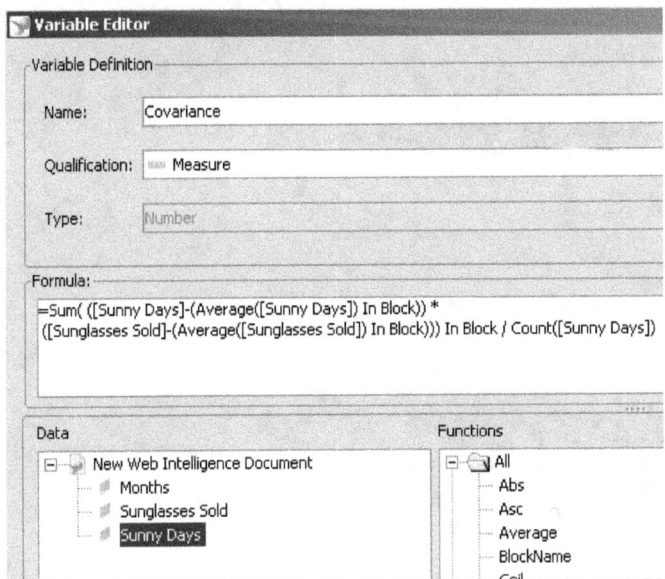

Code sample:

=Sum(([Sunny Days]-(Average([Sunny Days]) In Block)) *
([Sunglasses Sold]-(Average([Sunglasses Sold]) In Block))) In Block
/ Count([Sunny Days])

5. Create a variable called "Gradient" as shown below:

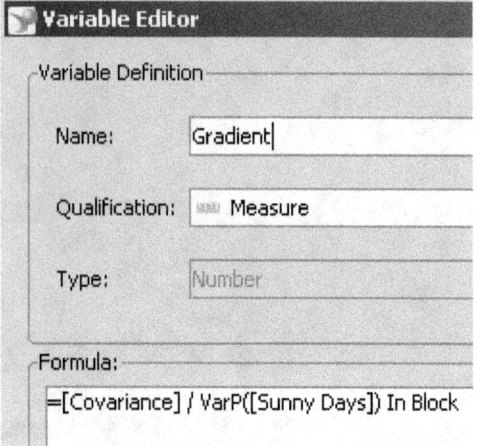

Code sample:

=[Covariance] / VarP([Sunny Days]) In Block

6. Create a variable called "Intercept" as shown below:

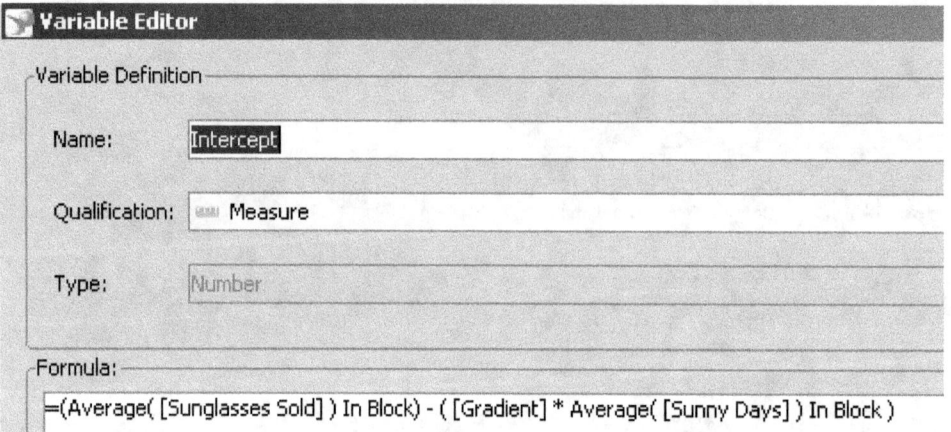

Code sample:

=(Average([Sunglasses Sold]) In Block) - ([Gradient] * Average([Sunny Days]) In Block)

7. Create a variable called "Correlation coefficient" as shown below:

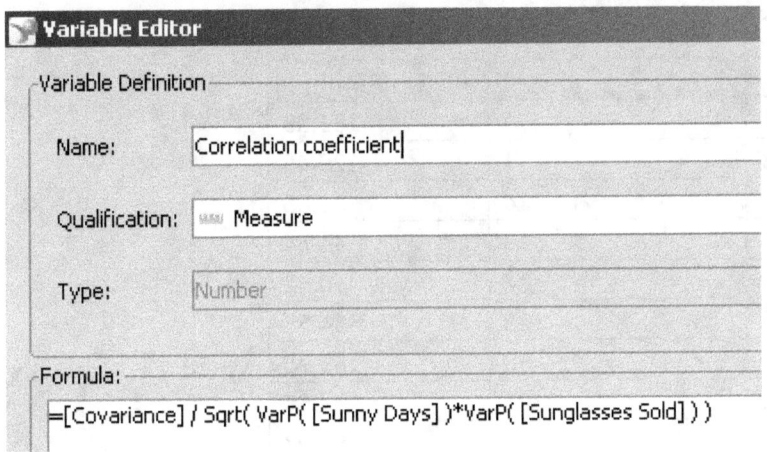

Code sample:

```
=[Covariance] / Sqrt( VarP( [Sunny Days] )*VarP( [Sunglasses Sold] ) )
```

8. Create a variable called "Regression line" as shown below:

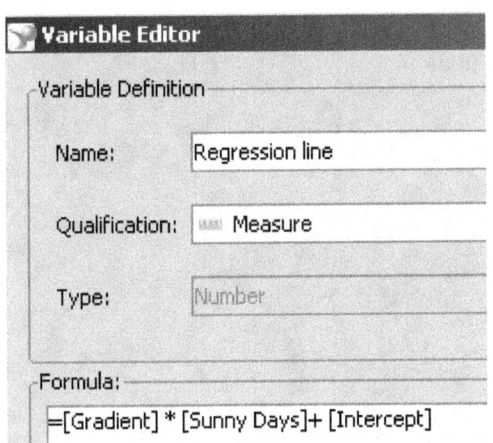

9. Drag and drop the variables you created into the cells underneath the "Sunglasses column" as shown in the schemas below.

Months	Sunny Days	Sunglasses Sold	Regression Line
January	1	1	-151.09
February	3	1	-129.45
March	12	14	-32.05
April	14	16	-10.4
May	15	17	0.42
June	20	25	54.53
July	30	30	162.75
August	31	301	173.58
September	29	20	151.93
October	20	15	54.53
November	12	11	-32.05
Decembre	10	9	-53.69
Gradient	0.93		
Coeficient corrélation	0.9		
Covariance	81.69		
Intercept	0.94		

A positive correlation coefficient of 0.9 indicates that an increase in the first variable would correspond to an increase in the second variable, thus implying a direct relationship between the variables.

A negative correlation would indicate an inverse relationship whereas one variable increases, the second variable decreases

MORE:

Linear regression equation: $Y = a + bx$

- b is the gradient, slope or regression coefficient
- a is the intercept of the line at Y axis or regression constant
- Y is a value for the outcome
- x is a value for the predictor

A positive correlation coefficient of 0.9 indicates that an increase in the first variable would correspond to an increase in the second variable, thus implying a direct relationship between the variables.

A negative correlation would indicate an inverse relationship whereas one variable increases, the second variable decreases

- The **linear regression** allows you to draw a chart illustrating the bound between sun glasses and sun, as well as establishing forecasts.

- The **gradient** will determine the degree to which the two variable's movements (sunny Days and Sun Glasses sales) are associated. The result 0.93 is an acceptable result, although 0.95 would have been better.

9. In order to start the creation of a chart related to the linear regression, remove all the columns with the exception of "Sunny Days" and "Regression line".

10. Right click the table, and select "turn to".

11. Select "vertical mixed line chart". The correct chart should be displayed as shown below:

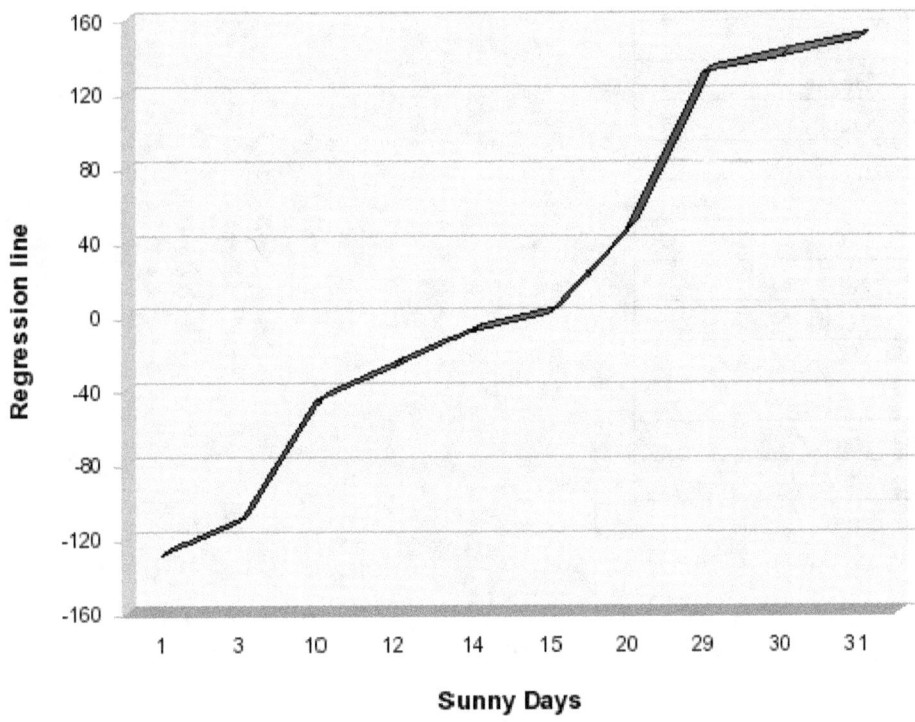

As the chart shows clearly, the points line up more or less in a straight line showing that there is a good correlation between the number of sun glasses sold and the number of sunny days.

Counting only valid records

Challenge | 19

🔍 Challenge

Business requirement: In this challenge you are requested to build a report providing the percentage of artists present in a total number of venues. You need to eliminate from this ratio the venues which don't have any artists allocated.

Artist	Cities
Madonna	Los Angeles
Madonna	Londres
Nicky Minaj	Berlin
Bruno Mars	Bruxelles
Taylor Swift	Geneva
NULL	Marseille
Eminem	Marseille
Drake	Liverpool
Madonna	New York
Madonna	Seattle
Madonna	New Orleans
NULL	Paris
NULL	Berlin
NULL	Madrid

Business justification: N/A

Business clue: You have been assigned the responsibility of creating in web intelligence a report obtaining the same output as in "Expected result.

Reference: On site experience.

🔍 Expected Result

- Bruno Mars should get 10% of the venues
- Drake should get 10% of the venues

- Eminem should get 10% of the venues
- Madonna should get 50% of the venues
- Madonna should get 50% of the venues
- Madonna should get 50% of the venues
- Madonna should get 50% of the venues
- Madonna should get 50% of the venues
- Nicky Minaj should get 10% of the venues
- Taylor Swift should get 10% of the venues

 ## Solution

The challenge here is to count only the artists names and to ignore the NULL values. The count function may not be the appropriate one to determine the total number of artists per venue.

1. Create a report based on the dimensions "Artists" and "Cities".

2. Create a measure "Grant total", drag and drop this measure into a column next to cities. This measure will sum each value "1" allocated to a non null artist.

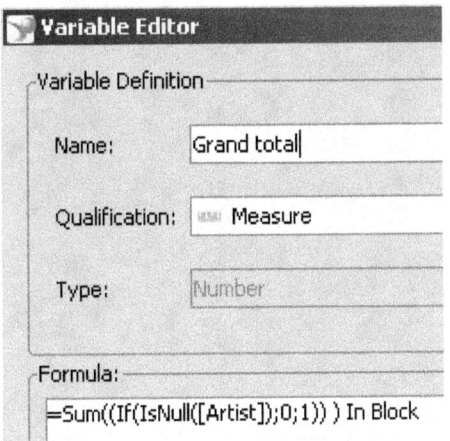

Code sample:

```
=Sum((If(IsNull([Artist]);0;1)) ) In Block
```

3. Create a measure "total per artist", drag and drop this measure into a column next to "Grant total".

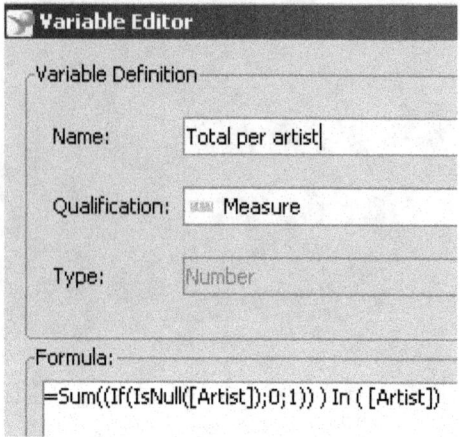

Code sample:

```
=Sum((If(IsNull([Artist]);0;1)) ) In ( [Artist])
```

3. Create a measure "Weight of each artist in total event", drag it and drop it into a column next to "Total per artist total".

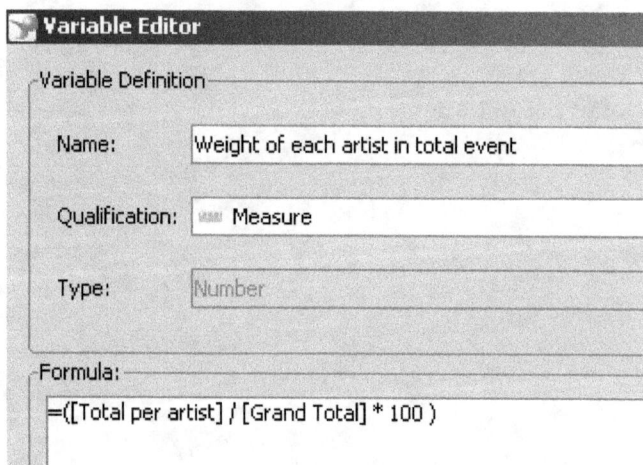

Code sample:

```
=([Total per artist] / [Grand Total] * 100 )
```

Ps: The same result as above might be reached by highlighting "Total per artist" and selecting the "%" functionality in the menu.

Artist	Cities	Total per artist	Weight of each artist in total event
Bruno Mars	Bruxelles	1	100%
DraKe	Liverpool	1	100%
Eminem	Marseille	1	100%
Madonna	Londres	5	50%
Madonna	Los Angeles	5	50%
Madonna	New Orleans	5	50%
Madonna	New YorK	5	50%
Madonna	Seattle	5	50%
NicKy Minaj	Berlin	1	100%
Taylor Swif	Geneva	1	100%

Adding a continental location to cities

Challenge | 20

 Challenge

Business requirement: In this challenge you are requested to use any appropriate trigram (EUR , USA) to represent the continental location of the cities found in the table below:

Artist	Cities
Madonna	Los Angeles
Madonna	Londres
Nicky Minaj	Berlin
Bruno Mars	Bruxelles
Taylor Swift	Geneva
NULL	Marseille
Eminem	Marseille
Drake	Liverpool
Madonna	New York
Madonna	Seattle
Madonna	New Orleans
NULL	Paris
NULL	Berlin
NULL	Madrid

Business justification: N/A

Business clue: You have been assigned the responsibility of creating in web intelligence a report obtaining the same output as shown in "Expected result.

Reference: N/A

 Expected Result

For example "Los Angeles" should be on the same row as "USA" and "Berlin" should be on the same row as "EUR".

Solution

1. Create a report based on "Artist" and "Cities".

2. Create a variable called "Zone". Create a column next to "Cities",

3. Drag and drop this variable into the new column.

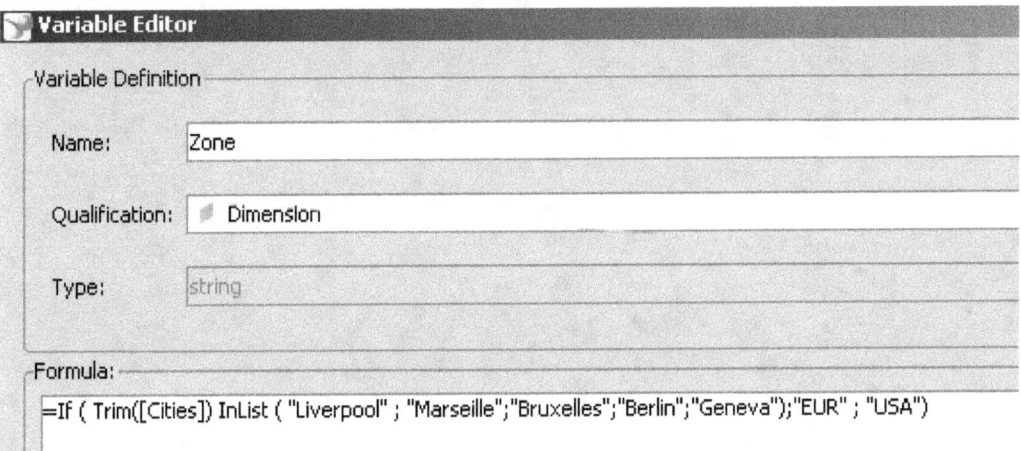

Code sample:

=If (Trim([Cities]) InList ("Liverpool" ; "Marseille";"Bruxelles";"Berlin";"Geneva");"EUR" ; "USA")

4. The output should appear as shown below:

Artist	Cities	Zone
Bruno Mars	Bruxelles	EUR
DraKe	Liverpool	EUR
Eminem	Marseille	EUR
Madonna	Londres	EUR
Madonna	Los Angeles	USA
Madonna	New Orleans	USA
Madonna	New YorK	USA
Madonna	Seattle	USA
NicKy Minaj	Berlin	EUR
TaylorSwif	Geneva	EUR

Highest quarterly sales for each year

Challenge | 21

Challenge

Business requirement: This challenge is based on the "efashion" universe and involves the dimensions "Year", "Quarter", "Month" and "Sales revenue".

You will be requested to extract the highest quarterly sales for each year.

Business justification: N/A

Business clue: You have been assigned the responsibility of creating in web intelligence a report obtaining the same output as in "Expected result".

Reference: This challenge is based on the "efashion" universe and involves the dimensions "Year", "Quarter", "Month" and "Sales revenue" with the records shown below.

Year	quarter	Month	Sale revenue
2004	Q1	1	$1,003,541
2004	Q1	2	$630,073
2004	Q1	3	$1,027,085
2004	Q2	4	$895,260
2004	Q2	5	$865,615
2004	Q2	6	$517.819
2004	Q3	7	$525.904
2004	Q3	8	$173.756
2004	Q3	9	$668,181
2004	Q4	10	$655,206
2004	Q4	11	$484.024
2004	Q4	12	$649,350
2005	Q1	1	$1,335,402
2005	Q1	2	$609,013
2005	Q1	3	$1,381,758

Year	Quarter	Month	Revenue
2005	Q2	4	$1.068,309
2005	Q2	5	$1,081,885
2005	Q2	6	$690,457
2005	Q3	7	$801,955
2005	Q3	8	$581.094
2005	Q3	9	$1,496,255
2005	Q4	10	$1.545.872
2005	Q4	11	$1,081,915
2005	Q4	12	$1.558,333
2006	Q1	1	$1,501,367
2006	Q1	2	$863,452
2006	Q1	3	$1,378.170
2006	Q2	4	$1,222.329
2006	Q2	5	$1,614,147
2006	Q2	6	$1.170,241
2006	Q3	7	$1,247.314
2006	Q3	8	$809,365
2006	Q3	9	$1,896,716
2006	Q4	10	$1,430,300
2006	Q4	11	$1,043,099
2006	Q4	12	$882,642

Expected Result

- For 2004, the first quarter (Q1) should appear with the highest income "$2660770".

- For 2005, the third quarter (Q4) should appear with the highest income "$418620".

- For 2006, the second quarter (Q2) should appear with the highest income "$4006718".

Solution

1. Create a report based on the dimension "Year", "Quarter", "Month", "Sales revenue".

2. Add a new column next to "Sales revenue".

3. Create the variable "Max quarterly revenue per year". Drag and drop this variable into the new column.

Variable Editor

Variable Definition

Name: Max quarterly revenue per year

Qualification: Measure

Type: Number

Formula:
=Max([Query 1].[Sales revenue] In ([Query 1].[Year];[Query 1].[Quarter])) In ([Query 1].[Year])

Code sample:

```
=Max([Query 1].[Sales revenue] In ([Query 1].[Year];[Query 1].[Quarter])) In ([Query 1].[Year])
```

5. The table below show only a partial result for 2004, with the best quarter being $2,660,700.

Year	Quarter	Month	Sales revenue	Highest Quarterly Sales Per year
2004	01	1	$1,003,541	$2,660,700
		2	$630,073	$2,660,700
		3	$1,027,085	$2,660,700
	01	Sum:	$2,660,700	
Year	**Quarter**	**Month**	**Sales revenue**	**Highest Quarterly Sales Per year**
	Q2	4	$895,260	$2,660,700
		5	$865,615	$2,660,700
		6	$517,819	$2,660,700
	Q2	Sum:	$2,278,693	
Year	**Quarter**	**Month**	**Sales revenue**	**Highest Quarterly Sales Per year**
	Q3	7	$525,904	$2,660,700
		8	$173,756	$2,660,700
		9	$668,181	$2,660,700
	Q3	Su	$1,367,841	

Highest monthly sale for each year

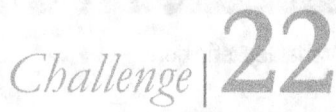

Challenge

Business requirement: This challenge is based on the "efashion" universe and involves the dimensions "Year", "Quarter", "Month" and "Sales revenue".

In this very specific example you will be requested to extract the highest monthly sale for each year.

Business justification: N/A

Business clue: You have been assigned the responsibility of creating in web intelligence a report obtaining the same output as in "Expected result".

Reference: Forums.

Expected Result

- For 2004, the highest monthly sale should be "$1027085".
- For 2005, the highest monthly sale should be "$1558333".
- For 2006, the highest monthly sale should be "$1896716".

Solution

1. Create a report based on the dimension "Year", "Quarter", "Month", "Sales revenue".

2. Add a new column next to "Sales revenue".

3. Create the variable "Highest monthly revenue per year". Drag and drop this variable into the new column.

Variable Editor

Variable Definition

Name: Highest monthly revenue per year

Qualification: Measure

Type: Number

Formula:
=Max([Query 1].[Sales revenue] In ([Query 1].[Year];[Query 1].[Quarter];[Query 1].[Month])) In ([Query 1].[Year])

Code sample:

```
=Max([Query 1].[Sales revenue] In ([Query 1].[Year];[Query 1].[Quarter];[Query 1].[Month])) In ([Query 1].[Year])
```

4. The result below is a partial result. We can see that for 2004 the highest month is "$1027085" and for 2005 the highest month is "$1558333".

   Regarding 2006, your report should indicate "$1896716".

Year	quarter	Month	Sale revenue	Highest monthly revenue per year
2004	Q1	1	$1,003,541	$1,027,085
2004	Q1	2	$630,073	$1,027,085
2004	Q1	3	$1,027,085	$1,027,085
2004	Q2	4	$895,260	$1,027,085
2004	Q2	5	$865,615	$1,027,085
2004	Q2	6	$517.819	$1,027,085
2004	Q3	7	$525.904	$1,027,085
2004	Q3	8	$173.756	$1,027,085
2004	Q3	9	$668,181	$1,027,085
2004	Q4	10	$655,206	$1,027,085
2004	Q4	11	$484.024	$1,027,085
2004	Q4	12	$649,350	$1,558,333
2005	Q1	1	$1,335,402	$1,558,333
2005	Q1	2	$609,013	$1,558,333
2005	Q1	3	$1,381,758	$1,558,333
2005	Q2	4	$1.068,309	$1,558,333

Year with the highest sale

Challenge | 23

 ## Challenge

Business requirement: The challenge is based on the "efashion" universe and involves the dimensions "Year", "Quarter", "Month" and "Sales revenue".

This challenge is a continuation of the previous challenge, but in this very specific example, you will be requested to extract the year with the highest sale.

Business justification: N/A

Business clue: You have been assigned the responsibility of creating in web intelligence a report obtaining the same output as in "Expected result".

Reference: Forums.

 ## Expected Result

The highest yearly sale should be 2006 with an income of "$15059143".

Solution

1. Create a report based on the dimension "Year", "Quarter", "Month", "Sales revenue".

2. Add a new column next to "Sales revenue".

3. Create the variable "Revenue per year".

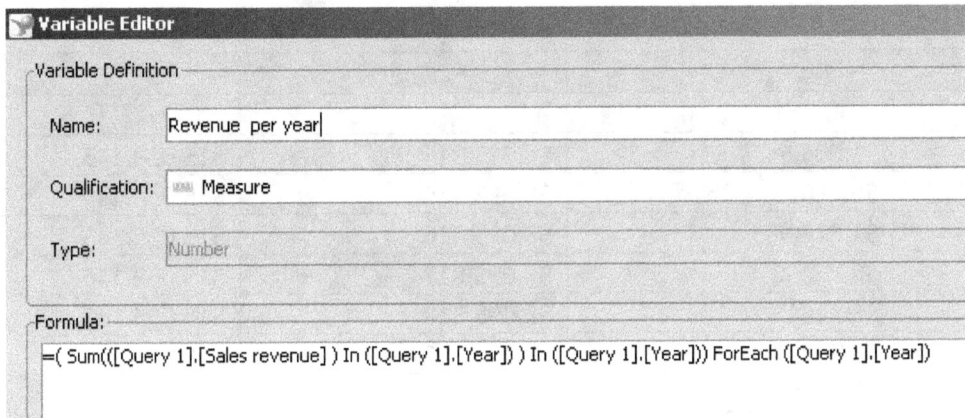

4. Drag and drop this variable into the new column

=(Sum((([Query 1].[Sales revenue]) In ([Query 1].[Year])) In ([Query 1].[Year]))
    ForEach ([Query 1].[Year]

5. Add a new column next to "Revenue per year".

6. Create a new variable "Max income per year".

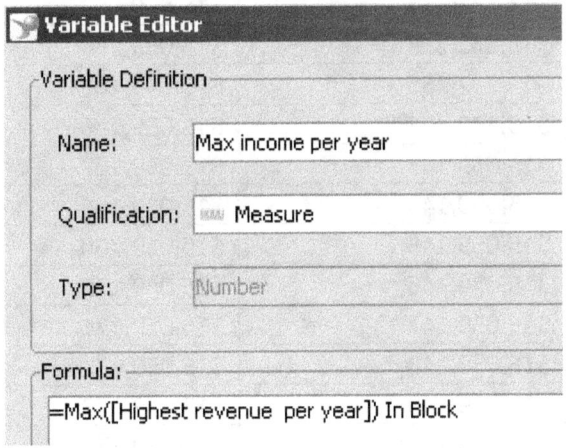

Code sample:

=Max([Highest revenue per year]) In Block

7. Drag and drop the **variable "Max income per year"** into the new column.

8. The year with the highest sale is 2006 with a total sale amount of "$15059143".

Year	quarter	Month	Sale revenue	Revenue per year	Max income per year
2004	Q1	1	$1,003,541	$8,095,814	$15,059,143
2004	Q1	2	$630,073	$8,095,815	$15,059,144
2004	Q1	3	$1,027,085	$8,095,816	$15,059,145
2004	Q2	4	$895,260	$8,095,817	$15,059,146
2004	Q2	5	$865,615	$8,095,818	$15,059,147
2004	Q2	6	$517.819	$8,095,819	$15,059,148
2004	Q3	7	$525.904	$8,095,820	$15,059,149
2004	Q3	8	$173.756	$8,095,821	$15,059,150
2004	Q3	9	$668,181	$8,095,822	$15,059,151
2004	Q4	10	$655,206	$8,095,823	$15,059,152
2004	Q4	11	$484.024	$8,095,824	$15,059,153
2004	Q4	12	$649,350	$8,095,825	$15,059,154
2005	Q1	1	$1,335,402	$13,232,246	$15,059,155
2005	Q1	2	$609,013	$13,232,247	$15,059,156
2005	Q1	3	$1,381,758	$13,232,248	$15,059,157
2005	Q2	4	$1.068,309	$13,232,249	$15,059,158
2005	Q2	5	$1,081,885	$13,232,250	$15,059,159
2005	Q2	6	$690,457	$13,232,251	$15,059,160
2005	Q3	7	$801,955	$13,232,252	$15,059,161
2005	Q3	8	$581.094	$13,232,253	$15,059,162
2005	Q3	9	$1,496,255	$13,232,254	$15,059,163
2005	Q4	10	$1.545.872	$13,232,255	$15,059,164
2005	Q4	11	$1,081,915	$13,232,256	$15,059,165
2005	Q4	12	$1.558,333	$13,232,257	$15,059,166
2006	Q1	1	$1,501,367	$15,059,143	$15,059,167
2006	Q1	2	$863,452	$15,059,144	$15,059,168
2006	Q1	3	$1,378.170	$15,059,145	$15,059,169
2006	Q2	4	$1,222.329	$15,059,146	$15,059,170
2006	Q2	5	$1,614,147	$15,059,147	$15,059,171
2006	Q2	6	$1.170,241	$15,059,148	$15,059,172
2006	Q3	7	$1,247.314	$15,059,149	$15,059,173
2006	Q3	8	$809,365	$15,059,150	$15,059,174
2006	Q3	9	$1,896,716	$15,059,151	$15,059,175
2006	Q4	10	$1,430,300	$15,059,152	$15,059,176
2006	Q4	11	$1,043,099	$15,059,153	$15,059,177
2006	Q4	12	$882,642	$15,059,154	$15,059,178

Highest monthly sale over three years

Challenge | 24

Challenge

Business requirement: The challenge is based on the "efashion" universe and involves the dimensions "Year", "Quarter"," Month" and "Sales revenue".

This challenge is a continuation of the previous challenge, but will explore the concept of extracting the "highest monthly sale over three years".

Business justification: N/A

Business clue: You have been assigned the responsibility of creating in web intelligence a report obtaining the same output as in "Expected result".

Reference: Forums.

Expected Result

The highest monthly sale over three years should be September 2006 with a total amount of "$1896716".

Solution

1. Create a report based on the dimension "Year", "Quarter", "Month", "Sales revenue".

2. Add a new column next to "Sales revenue".

3. Create the variable "Highest monthly revenue per year".

4. Drag and drop this variable into the new column.

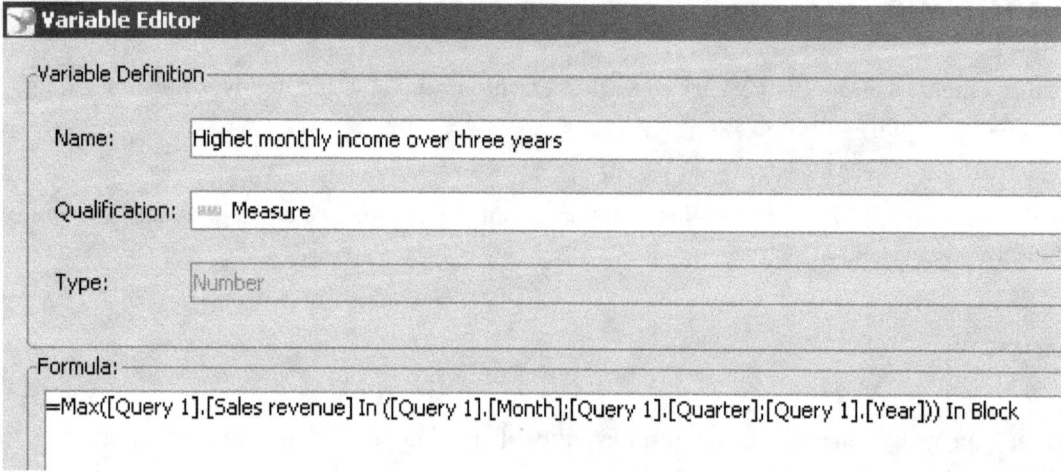

Code sample:

```
=Max([Query 1].[Sales revenue] In ([Query 1].[Month];[Query 1].[Quarter];[Query 1].[Year])) In Block
```

5. The highest monthly sale over three years is September 2006 with a total amount of "$1896716".

6. As a final result you should get the result below.

Year	Quarter	Month	Sale revenue	Highest Monthly Sale
2005	4	10	$1,545,872	$1,896,716
2005	4	11	$1,081,915	$1,896,716
2005	4	12	$1,558,333	$1,896,716
2006	1	1	$1,501,367	$1,896,716
2006	1	2	$863,452	$1,896,716
2006	2	3	$1,378,170	$1,896,716
2006	2	4	$1,222,329	$1,896,716
2006	2	5	$1,614,147	$1,896,716
2006	2	6	$1,170,241	$1,896,716
2006	3	7	$1,247,314	$1,896,716
2006	3	8	$809,365	$1,896,716
2006	3	9	$1,896,716	$1,896,716
2006	4	10	$1,430,300	$1,896,716
2006	4	11	$1,043,009	$1,896,716
2006	4	12	$882,642	$1,896,716

Highest quarterly sale over three years

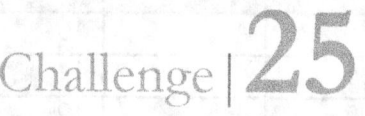

 ## Challenge

This challenge will be the last of the series. It is still based on the "efashion" universe and involves the dimensions "Year", "Quarter", "Month" and "Sales Revenue". The goal of this challenge is to extract the highest quarterly sale over three years.

Business requirement:

This challenge will be the last of the series. It is still based on the "efashion" universe and involves the dimensions "Year", "Quarter", "Month" and "Sales Revenue". The goal of this challenge is to extract the highest quarterly sale over three years.

Business justification: N/A

Business clue: You have been assigned the responsibility of creating in web intelligence a report obtaining the same output as in "Expected result".

Reference: Forums.

 ## Expected Result

The highest quarterly sale over three years should be 2005 / Q4 with a total amount of "$4186120".

 ## Solution

1. Create a report based on the dimension "Year", "Quarter", "Month", "Sales Revenue".

2. Add a new column next to "Sales Revenue".

3. Create the variable "Highest monthly revenue per year".

4. Drag and drop this variable into the new column.

Variable Editor

Variable Definition

Name: Highest quartely income over three years

Qualification: Measure

Type: Number

Formula:
=Max([Query 1].[Sales revenue] In ([Query 1].[Quarter];[Query 1].[Year])) In Block

Code sample:

```
=Max([Query 1].[Sales revenue] In ([Query 1].[Quarter];[Query 1].[Year])) In Block
```

5. The highest quarterly income over three years is 2005 / Q4 with a total amount of "$4186120".

Year	Quarter	Sales revenue	Highest quarterly income over three years
2004	Q1	$2,660,700	$4,186,120
2004	Q2	$2,278,693	$4,186,121
2004	Q3	$1,367,841	$4,186,122
2004	Q4	$1,788,580	$4,186,123
2005	Q1	$3,326,172	$4,186,124
2005	Q2	$2,840,651	$4,186,125
2005	Q3	$2,879,303	$4,186,126
2005	Q4	$4,186,120	$4,186,127
2006	Q1	$3,742,988	$4,186,128

www.ingramcontent.com/pod-product-compliance
Lightning Source LLC
Chambersburg PA
CBHW080948170526
45158CB00008B/2410